REVISE FOR

SCIENCE GCSE

MEG COORDINATED

GILL ALDERTON
DAVID BERRINGTON
MICHAEL BRIMICOMBE

FOUNDATION

Heinemann Educational Publishers
Halley Court, Jordan Hill, Oxford, OX2 8EJ
a division of Reed Educational & Professional Publishing Ltd

Heinemann is a registered trademark of Reed Educational &
Professional Publishing Ltd.

OXFORD   MELBOURNE   AUCKLAND
JOHANNESBURG   BLANTYRE   GABORONE
IBADAN   PORTSMOUTH NH (USA)   CHICAGO

© Gill Alderton, David Berrington, Michael Brimicombe, 1998

First published 1998

ISBN 0 435 57867 7

02 01 00 99 98
10 9 8 7 6 5 4 3 2 1

Edited by June Thompson

Designed and typeset by Ken Vail Graphic Design

Illustrated by Ken Vail Graphic Design,
Graham-Cameron Illustration (Virginia Gray)

Cover artwork by Stephen May

Printed and bound in Great Britain by The Bath Press

Contents

How to use this book

This book is divided into three sections:

- AT2 (biology)
- AT3 (chemistry)
- AT4 (physics)

Helping you revise

1   At the end of each chapter is a *Concept map*. This will help you check that you remember everything you need to know and will help you see the connections between topics more clearly.

   The best plan is to make your own personal map of the subject which makes your own connections between topics.

2   The words in **bold** are all key words you need to know. A useful revision idea would be to build up your own glossary of these as you work through the book. For quick reference to a word or topic use the *Index* at the back of the book.

3   There are lots of questions in the book and they are an important part of your revision. There are:

   - simple questions to help you stop and think about the subject as you read.
   - questions at the end of each section to help you practise for the exam.

   The answers to all these are at the back of the book so you will never get stuck.

Good luck with your exams!

AT2

Life Processes and Living Things

The basics of life

The seven signs of life

All living things carry out the following **seven** activities. This makes them different from non-living things.

1 **M**ovement – animals move their whole bodies, plants move as they grow.
2 **R**eproduction – they make new individuals like themselves.
3 **S**ensitivity – they are aware of, and can respond to changes in their surroundings.
4 **G**rowth – they all get bigger.
5 **R**espiration – they release energy from their food.
6 **E**xcretion – they get rid of waste products they have made.
7 **F**eeding – animals eat, plants make their own food by photosynthesis in their leaves.

Now do this

1 The first letters of each activity make the words 'Mrs Gref'. Cover the list and use 'Mrs Gref' to help you write down all of the activities.

2 Which of the following are living things: coal, wood, plastic, maggots, grass, feathers, an oak tree and a sausage?

The building blocks of life

All living things are made of cells. These are so tiny that you can only see them using a microscope.

Cells contain:
• a **nucleus** to control everything a cell does
• **cytoplasm** – a watery jelly in which most of the cell's reactions take place
• a **cell membrane** which controls what goes in and out of the cell
• **mitochondria** which release energy from food (respiration).

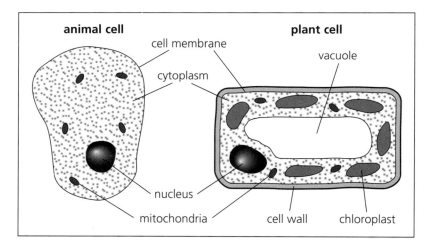

Plant cells also have a few extras!
• a **cellulose cell wall** to help support the plant – think of the size of tall trees, and remember they don't have any bones to hold them up
• **chloroplasts** to contain the chlorophyll needed for photosynthesis
• large **cell vacuole**, a space filled with a fluid called cell sap.

The main chemical in cells is water.

Substances in cells
inorganic – minerals and water
organic – carbohydrates
– fats and oils
– amino acids and proteins
– nucleic acid (DNA)

The right cell for the job

Cells contain the same basic parts, but they also have important differences. They are specialised to do different jobs. For example:

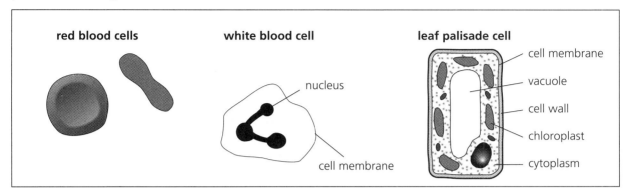

Red blood cells carry oxygen. They have no nucleus to make more space in the cell for carrying oxygen.
White blood cells fight infection and so they can change their shape to surround and eat microbes.

Leaf palisade cells are close to the surface of leaves. They are long and thin with lots of chloroplasts to trap light for photosynthesis. This diagram shows where the pallisade cells are found in the leaf.

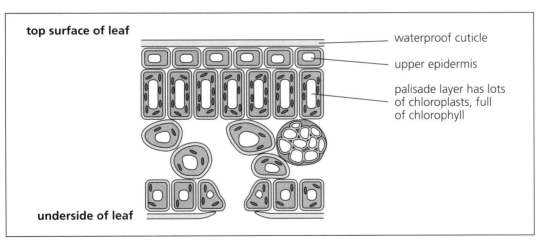

 Now do this

3 Which part of a plant cell
   a is needed for photosynthesis
   b controls what moves in and out of the cell
   c supports the plant?

4 What **four** things do both plant and animal cells have?

Digestion

The food you eat has to reach all your cells. To do this, it has to be broken down so that it can be carried in the blood. Large insoluble molecules are broken down into small soluble molecules. This breaking down is called **digestion**.

The digestive system

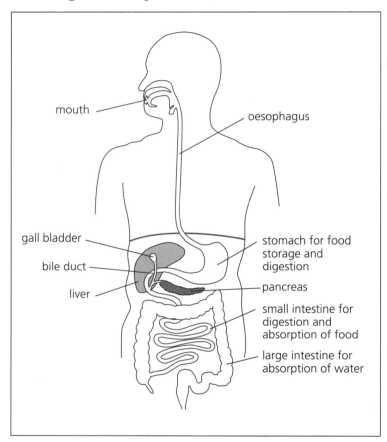

mouth

oesophagus

gall bladder

bile duct

liver

stomach for food storage and digestion

pancreas

small intestine for digestion and absorption of food

large intestine for absorption of water

 Now do this

1 What is digestion?
2 Name **two** parts of the digestive system where digestion occurs.
3 Where is the digested food absorbed?
4 What is absorbed in the large intestine?

Moving food through the system

Food is squeezed through the digestive system by the circular muscles in the walls of the oesophagus, stomach and intestines. This squeezing action is called **peristalsis**.

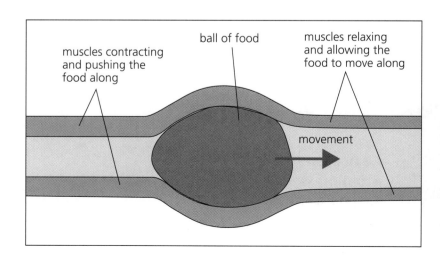

muscles contracting and pushing the food along

ball of food

muscles relaxing and allowing the food to move along

movement

Breaking down food

As the food moves along it is worked on by **enzymes**. Enzymes are **catalysts** made of protein. They speed up the breakdown of the large molecules in the food into small molecules. The small molecules can then be carried in the blood. Different types of enzymes break down different foods.

Types of enzyme	What they do	Where they work
amylase	breaks down starch to maltose (sugar)	mouth and small intestine
protease	breaks down proteins to amino acids	stomach and small intestine
lipase	breaks down fats to fatty acids and glycerol	small intestine

The enzyme found in the stomach needs acid conditions to work well. So the stomach makes an acid to provide the right conditions. The acid also kills any microbes in the food (sterilises the food).

Absorbing the food

Food is **absorbed** in the small intestine. The food molecules are now small enough to pass through the intestine wall into the blood. To speed this up the walls of the small intestine are folded into many **villi** which make a greater surface area for food molecules to pass through.

One villus, lots of villi

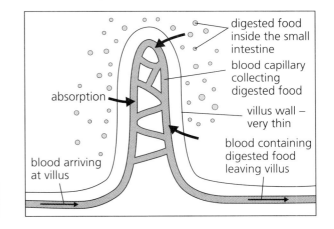

digested food inside the small intestine

blood capillary collecting digested food

villus wall – very thin

blood containing digested food leaving villus

absorption

blood arriving at villus

Testing foods

You can find out what molecules are in different foods by carrying out the simple tests shown in the table.

Starch	Add iodine solution	A blue/black colour shows starch
Protein	Add biuret solution	A mauve colour shows protein
Simple sugars	Add Benedict's solution and then warm	A brick red colour shows a simple sugar
Fats	Rub on a piece of paper Add ethanol to the food and the same amount of water. Shake well.	Look for a grease spot Look for a cloudy white colour

Now do this

5 How do enzymes help with digestion?

6 Give **two** uses of stomach acid.

7 Name **two** parts of the digestive system that produce enzymes.

Breathing

Your body cells use food for the energy they need (in **respiration**). To release this energy they need oxygen. As well as energy, carbon dioxide, a waste product, is released.

Amount of gas entering and leaving the body		
Gas	air in	air out
Oxygen	21%	16%
Carbon dioxide	0.04%	4%

The oxygen you need comes from the air you breathe in to your lungs. In your lungs oxygen enters your blood. Blood carries oxygen to all your cells. Your blood also collects the waste carbon dioxide from your cells and takes it back to your lungs where it passes out into the air. This is called **gas exchange**.

One air sac is called an alveolus, lots are called alveoli.

Your lungs

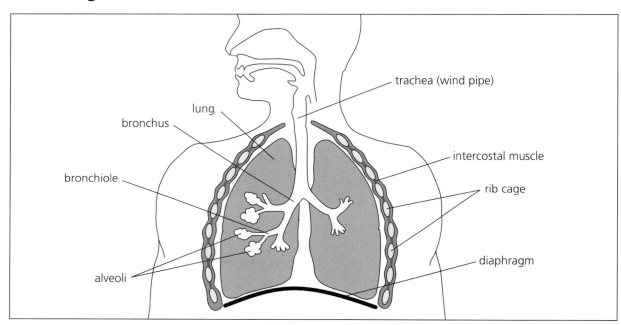

The air enters your lungs through the **trachea** (windpipe). This branches into the **bronchus** and then into **bronchioles** which carry air deep into the lungs. At the end of the bronchioles are lots of little air sacs called **alveoli** where gas exchange takes place.

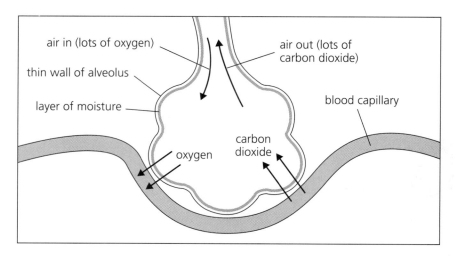

When you breathe in, there is a lot of oxygen (a high **concentration**) in the alveoli. There is very little oxygen (a low concentration) in the blood in the capillaries. So oxygen moves from the alveoli into the blood by **diffusion**.

The lungs are good at gas exchange because they have:
- a large surface area (thousands of alveoli)
- moist surfaces which make diffusion faster
- thin walled alveoli which make diffusion faster
- lots of blood capillaries to carry the gases.

 ### Now do this

1   Blood coming back to the lungs has a higher concentration of carbon dioxide than the air in the alveoli. How does carbon dioxide pass from the blood into the alveoli?

2   Your lungs look pink because they have such a lot of blood capillaries in them. Why do lungs need so much blood?

Breathing

Two things happen when you breathe in:
- your intercostal muscles between your ribs contract and this makes your rib cage move up and out
- your diaphragm contracts and flattens downwards.

This makes the space inside your rib cage bigger and the air pressure drops. This sucks air into your lungs from outside.

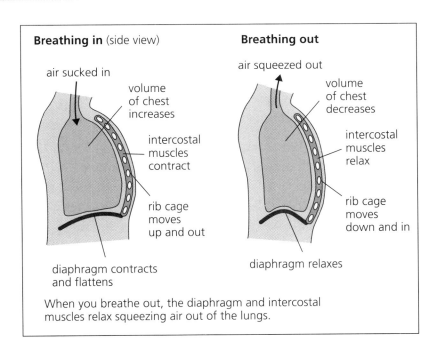

Breathing in (side view)

air sucked in

volume of chest increases

intercostal muscles contract

rib cage moves up and out

diaphragm contracts and flattens

Breathing out

air squeezed out

volume of chest decreases

intercostal muscles relax

rib cage moves down and in

diaphragm relaxes

When you breathe out, the diaphragm and intercostal muscles relax squeezing air out of the lungs.

 ### Now do this

3   Put your hands on your rib cage while you breathe in. Now describe what you can feel and why this pulls air into your lungs.

4   Look at the diagram showing how we breathe. Now explain how we breathe out.

Circulation

Your body has a **transport system**. It carries materials such as oxygen and food to all the body cells. It also carries waste products such as carbon dioxide away from the body cells. There are three main parts.

1 A liquid called **blood** to carry the materials.
2 A network of tubes called **blood vessels**.
3 A pump, called the **heart**.

Blood

Blood is made up of :

- **plasma** – a watery liquid which transports foods, water, hormones and waste products such as urea and carbon dioxide

- **red blood cells** which transport oxygen around the body

- **white blood cells** which defend the body against disease

- **platelets** which help blood to clot if the skin is torn.

Now do this

1 Which part of the blood carries oxygen around the body?

2 What is the job of platelets?

Blood vessels

The blood is carried around the body in blood vessels. There are **three** different types of blood vessel.

1 **Arteries** carry blood away from the heart. This blood is at a high pressure because of the pumping of the heart.
2 **Veins** carry blood at a lower pressure back to the heart.
3 **Capillaries** are very small vessels which link arteries and veins and allow the substances which the blood carries like food, water and gases to move in and out of body cells.

Leaking capillaries

Capillaries have very thin walls with little holes which allow plasma to leak out and become **tissue fluid**. Tissue fluid surrounds the body cells so that food and oxygen can diffuse into the cells from the tissue fluid and waste materials can diffuse out of the cells. The tissue fluid then returns to the capillary.

Now do this

3 Name the **three** different types of blood vessel.

4 Which blood vessels carry blood away from the heart?

5 Which blood vessels contain blood at high pressure?

The heart

Blood has to be pumped around the body, and this is the job of the heart.

The heart is made of muscle. It contains **four chambers** and **four valves**.

One atrium,
two atria

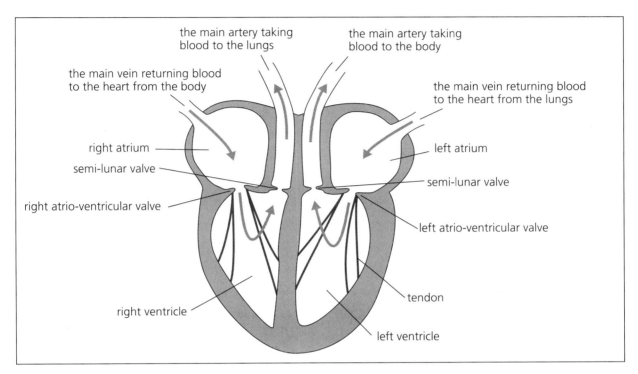

The right atrium and left atrium collect blood coming in from the veins. The right and left ventricles contract to squirt blood out into the arteries at high pressure. High pressure is needed because some of the blood has a long way to go.

The arrows show the direction of blood flow. The valves stop the blood flowing backwards.

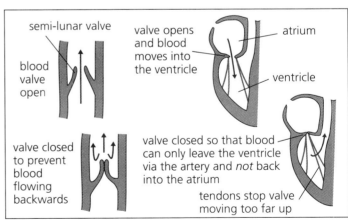

Now do this

6 What is the job of the heart?

7 Name the **four** chambers of the heart.

8 Why is it necessary to have valves in the heart?

Senses and the nervous system

We are aware of and can respond to changes in our surroundings. These changes are called **stimuli** and they are detected by parts of our bodies called **receptors**.

Receptors are part of our **sense organs**.
Sense organs detect stimuli:
- ears detect sound and balance
- eyes detect light
- noses detect chemicals (smell)
- tongues detect chemicals (taste)
- skin detects touch, pressure and temperature change.

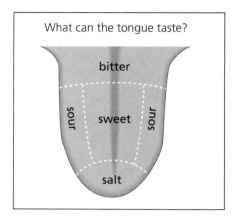

What can the tongue taste?

bitter

sour   sweet   sour

salt

The eye

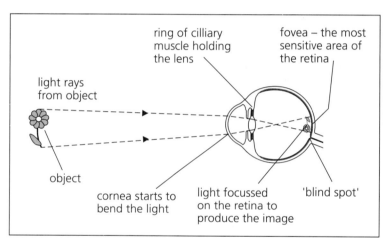

ring of cilliary muscle holding the lens

fovea – the most sensitive area of the retina

light rays from object

object

cornea starts to bend the light

light focussed on the retina to produce the image

'blind spot'

Now do this

1 Unscramble the letters to find which stimulus goes with these sense organs:

DUSON; TLGIH; SSRPEUER; SCCMLHEIA; EMRPETRTUEA

skin   ear
eye   nose

Light from the object reaches the cornea. The cornea bends the light as it passes through. The lens bends the light a little more to produce a clear focussed image.

Now do this

2 Complete the table.

Name	Function
retina	detects the light stimulus
iris	
	changes shape to bend the light
optic nerve	

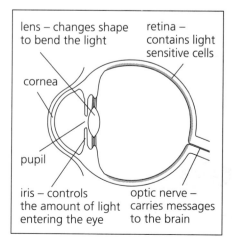

lens – changes shape to bend the light

retina – contains light sensitive cells

cornea

pupil

iris – controls the amount of light entering the eye

optic nerve – carries messages to the brain

Fast response

We often need to react to stimuli. For example, if you pick up a hot plate which burns you, you quickly drop it. For this we need our body to act on information from receptors and this is the job of the **central nervous system**.

The central nervous system is made up of the brain and spinal cord. It is connected to all the parts of the body by a network of nerve cells called peripheral nerves.

There are two types of nerve cells or **neurones**. Messages coming into the central nervous system from the sense organs travel along **sensory neurones**. Nerve cells carrying messages away from the CNS are called **motor neurones**.

The sensory and motor neurones have different shapes. Neurones are long and thin to carry messages over long distances.

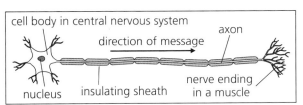

A motor neurone

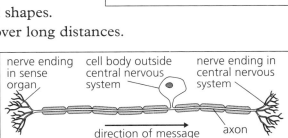

A sensory neurone

Reflex actions

What actually happens when you touch something hot?

1 Temperature receptors in your skin detect the hot stimulus.
2 They send the message along a sensory neurone to the central nervous system.
3 The central nervous system sends the message along a motor neurone to a muscle (an **effector**).
4 The muscle contracts and moves your hand away from the hot object.

This is called a reflex action. It happens very fast and without you having to think about it. Reflex actions are often protective. The pathways can be shown like this:

stimulus → receptor → sensory → central → motor → effector → response
                      neurone   nervous   neurone (muscle)
                                 system

Now do this

3 If a ball comes flying towards your eyes but it doesn't hit you, you blink. Write a nerve pathway to show how this happens. Add the names of the parts involved where you know them (e.g. the receptor is the retina).

Hormones

Some reactions that take place in our bodies are controlled by **hormones**. These are chemical messengers produced by groups of cells called **glands**. They travel in the blood plasma to their **target cells**. Each hormone acts in a particular way on its specific target cells.

Controlling sugar levels

Sugar is needed by all your cells for energy. It is very important to have the right amount of available sugar in your blood. Too much or too little can be dangerous.

The amount of sugar in your blood is controlled by a hormone called **insulin**, which is produced by the pancreas. When there is too much sugar in the blood, the pancreas releases insulin which lowers the level of sugar.

Some people do not make insulin or do not make enough. This means that they suffer from **diabetes** and the level of sugar in their blood can go up and down dramatically. Many diabetics can control their blood sugar level by injecting themselves with insulin.

Controlling sexual development

The changes which take place during adolescence as children grow into adults are controlled by sex hormones.

As girls grow older their ovaries start to produce **oestrogen**. Oestrogen causes a number of changes in girls. They: ▶

- start their menstrual cycle (have periods)
- develop breasts
- grow pubic and underarm hair
- grow taller.

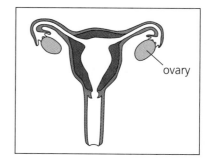

These are called **secondary sexual characteristics**.

In boys, the development of secondary sexual characteristics is controlled by **testosterone** which is produced by the testes. Under the effect of testosterone boys: ▶

- grow taller
- develop longer penises
- grow pubic, underarm and facial hair
- develop deeper voices.

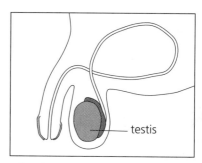

Glands producing sex hormones

Now do this

1 What is a hormone?

2 Where are hormones made?

3 Explain how insulin injections help a diabetic.

4 Describe the secondary sexual characteristics controlled by **a** oestrogen and **b** testosterone.

Controlling the menstrual cycle

There are two hormones involved in controlling a woman's menstrual cycle: **oestrogen** and **progesterone**.

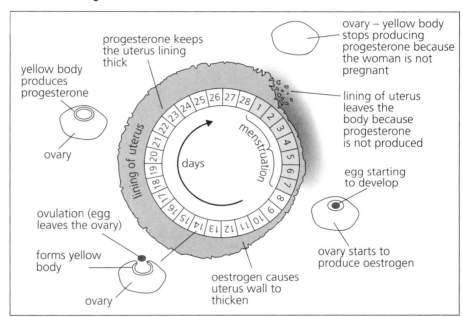

Preventing pregnancy...

Hormones can be used in **contraceptive pills** to prevent the ovaries releasing eggs. This means that a woman cannot get pregnant.

...and helping pregnancy

Some women have difficulty in getting pregnant. Hormones can be used to help them produce more eggs which will increase their chances of getting pregnant.

 Now do this

5 Explain why a pregnant woman will not normally menstruate.

6 How does a contraceptive pill work?

7 What part does oestrogen play in the menstrual cycle?

Control in plants

Plants do not have a nervous system and so usually cannot respond as quickly as animals. They react to their surroundings more slowly. Their reactions are controlled by hormones called **auxins**. These are dissolved in water to allow them to move through the plant.

Auxins control:
- growth of shoots and roots
- flowering
- ripening of fruit.

How do plants grow?

The shoots of a plant always grow towards the light. This is very important because the leaves need as much light as possible to make food for the plant by photosynthesis.

Plant roots always grow downwards under the effect of gravity. Again, this is very important for finding the water which the plant needs and for anchoring the plant in the ground.

 Now do this

1 Why does it take longer for hormones in a plant to produce an effect than for the nervous system in an animal?

Auxins control the direction that plants grow in by making different parts grow at different speeds. To make a shoot grow towards the light they make its shaded side grow faster so that the tip bends over towards the light. To make a root that has just emerged grow downwards they stop the under side of the root growing so that the tip curves downwards.

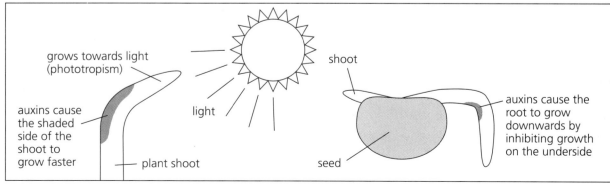

grows towards light (phototropism)

shoot

light

auxins cause the shaded side of the shoot to grow faster

plant shoot

seed

auxins cause the root to grow downwards by inhibiting growth on the underside

122

EDNA
SCIENCE
single sided
15 copies of each
please a.s.a.p.
IN SETS please

Using plant hormones

We use synthetic (man-made) auxins to trick plants and make them behave in ways which are more convenient for us.

1 Making more plants

It can take some time for plants to produce young new plants naturally. Gardeners speed up the process by cutting shoots off plants and dipping them in auxins to make them grow roots. These auxins are called rooting powder.

2 Slowing fruit ripening

Auxins can also be used to slow down fruit ripening. This is useful for farmers who have a long way to take their fruit to the shops. If farmers treat it in this way it stops the fruit getting overripe before it gets to customers.

3 Selective weedkillers

Selective weedkillers contain auxins which speed up the growth of selected plants. This makes them grow too fast and then they quickly die. For example, if there are weeds with broad leaves growing in a lawn a weedkiller can be used which will kill only those weeds not the grass.

Have you ever thought how seedless grapes and oranges are made? If you apply auxins to flowers before they are pollinated they will grow into fruit without any seeds.

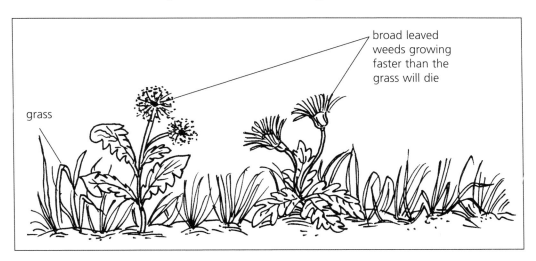

broad leaved weeds growing faster than the grass will die

grass

🎲 *Now do this*

2 What is auxin?

3 Name **two** stimuli that plants respond to.

4 Describe **two** commercial uses of auxins.

5 Explain what is meant by a 'selective' weedkiller.

Ecosystems

Ecology is the study of living things and the way they interact with each other and with their surroundings (**environment**).

To make it easier to study the environment, it is divided into lots of smaller areas called **ecosystems**. For example, a rock pool is an ecosystem.

Every ecosystem is made up of **two** parts:

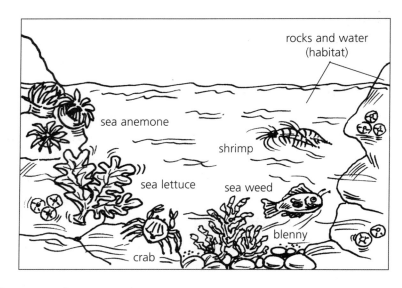

- **habitat**, – which is the non-living part, for example the water and rocks in the rock pool
- **community**, which is the living part, made up of the **populations** of plants and animals. A population includes all members of the same species. In the rock pool there might be a population of crabs, a population of sea anemone, a population of sea lettuce and many more.

Don't forget the plants! They are living things and are therefore part of the community.

 Now do this

Look at the bottle garden. It is an example of a man-made ecosystem.

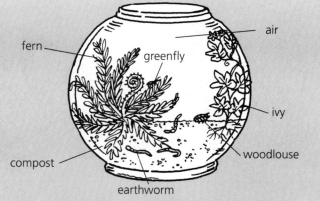

1   What are the **two** main parts of the habitat in the bottle garden?

2   Name **four** species which form part of the community in the bottle garden.

3   Suggest what might happen to the bottle garden ecosystem if the plants all died.

4   Suggest **three** other ecosystems.

Grouping living things

There is such a wide variety of living things, that scientists have divided them into smaller groups in order to study them.

Members of a group have a number of things in common. For example, all animals with a backbone can be divided into:

- **fish** – scales, fins, gills and live in water
- **amphibia** – breed in water, have a soft, moist skin
- **reptiles** – can lay eggs away from water, dry skin with scales
- **birds** – feathers and wings
- **mammals** – hair or fur, feed their young on milk.

Scientists then use **keys** to identify where each living thing belongs. A key is a set of questions. The questions are based on things you can see. You have to look at the first question and compare it with your living thing. Answer the question, yes or no. How you answer the questions will lead you through the key.

Now do this

5 Use the key to identify organisms A, B, C, D and E.

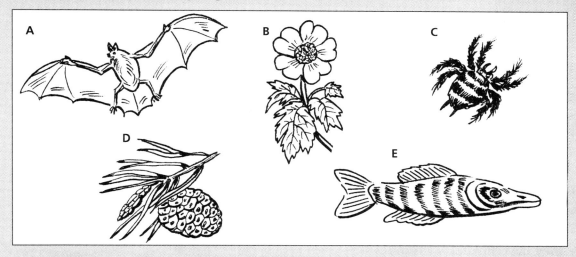

i Is it a plant?........................ Yes, go to Qii.
.... No, go to Qiii.

ii Is it a flowering plant? .... Yes, buttercup.
.... No, Scots pine.

iii Does it have legs? .... Yes, go to Qiv.
.... No, pike.

iv Does it have 8 legs? .... Yes, tarantula.
.... No, pipistrelle.

Surviving the environment

To survive in an environment, living things need:

- water
- space
- light
- minerals
- food
- shelter.

The size of a population depends on how much of these requirements is available. For example, sunflower seedlings growing together in a single pot will not grow as big and strong as the sunflower seedlings grown in individual pots.

When a population becomes too large for the resources in its surroundings it stops growing. Living things also compete against each other for these resources. The size of a population usually depends on how well it competes against other populations for what it needs.

If wheat is planted close together the yield is increased because more wheat plants fit into a field. But if the plants are too close together they compete for space, water and light and do not grow so well, resulting in reduced yield.

Adaptating to survive

Each population is **adapted** to survive in its particular habitat. For example:

1 Polar bears are adapted to very cold habitats. They have:
   - a thick layer of fat to insulate from the cold
   - a thick coat of fur to keep body heat in
   - a large body so less heat is lost to the air.

thick fur coat

white for camouflage against snow

2 Fish are adapted to survive in water. They are:
   - streamlined to move easily through the water
   - they have waterproof scales
   - they have fins for swimming
   - they have gills for gas exchange.

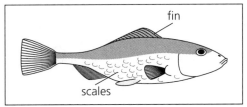

fin

scales

Now do this

1 Make separate lists of **four** things animals and plants need to survive.

2 Suggest why goldfish usually grow bigger in a garden pond than they do in a goldfish bowl.

3 Give **three** ways in which a polar bear is adapted to live in a cold area.

Plants are also adapted to survive. For example, small plants on woodland floors, such as bluebells, flower very early before the leaves grow on the trees and block the light from the Sun. Many plants also have to protect themselves against animals to survive. They use spines, stings or poisons to avoid being eaten.

Predators are animals which eat other animals (**prey**). Predators are more likely to catch their prey if they:
- are **camouflaged** and difficult to see, like a polar bear in the snow
- have large teeth, claws, sting or poison to kill their 'food'
- have good senses – sight, hearing or smell – to find the 'food'.

Prey try to escape being caught by:
- camouflage so they are hard to see, like a stick insect
- colours which warn that they are unpleasant to eat like yellow and black wasps
- tasting horrible – predators soon learn which caterpillars are tasty.

Predators depend upon prey so if the numbers of prey in a habitat go down, then some predators will starve and the number of predators will also go down.

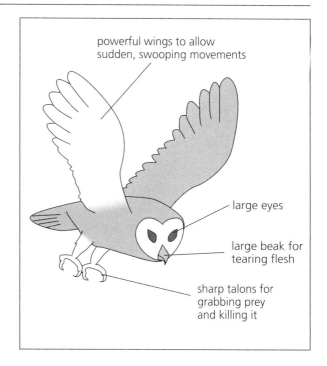

powerful wings to allow sudden, swooping movements

large eyes

large beak for tearing flesh

sharp talons for grabbing prey and killing it

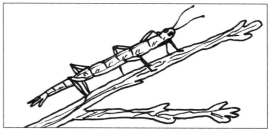

 Now do this

4   Name a predator and give **three** ways it is adapted to be a predator.

5   Name a prey species and give **three** ways it is adapted to survive.

6   If the number of prey decreases, what will happen to the number of predators?

7   Read the following passage.
    Field mice live in fields of wheat. They form an important part of the diet of a barn owl. Barn owls fly low looking for their prey and as the number of cars has increased, so too has the number of owls killed by flying into cars.
    a Name the predator mentioned in this passage.
    b Explain what effect an increase in traffic might have on the amount of wheat the farmer would get from his field.

Food chains

All animals depend on plants for their food. Even animals which don't eat plants directly will eat animals which have eaten plants. Animals which eat plants are called **herbivores**. Animals which eat meat are called **carnivores**. Animals which eat both are called **omnivores**.

Green plants make their own food (glucose and starches) using energy from the Sun. They are called **producers** because they make (produce) their own food. Other living things are called **consumers** because they have to get their food by eating (consuming) green plants or other animals.

These feeding relationships can be drawn as a **food chain**. Some of the energy captured from light by plants is passed down the food chain as plants and animals are eaten.

The arrows **must** point towards the animal that is eating because it shows the direction the energy is moving in.

grass → rabbit, means the rabbit eats the grass

grass ← rabbit, means the grass eats the rabbit!!

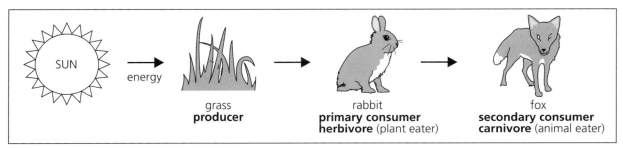

SUN → energy	grass **producer**	rabbit **primary consumer** **herbivore** (plant eater)	fox **secondary consumer** **carnivore** (animal eater)

Pyramids of numbers

Another way of showing feeding relationships is as a **pyramid of numbers**. Here, each feeding level is represented by a block. The size of the block represents the number of individuals.

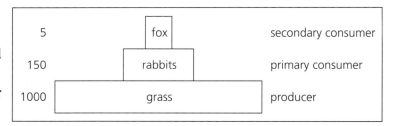

5	fox	secondary consumer
150	rabbits	primary consumer
1000	grass	producer

 Now do this

1 On a moorland the main plant is heather which is eaten by lots of animals including rabbits, grouse, bees and deer. There are also several fox families and a pair of eagles which survive by hunting the grouse and rabbits.
   a Name one moorland producer, one primary consumer and one predator.
   b Draw **two** food chains using some of the living things mentioned in the passage.
   c Draw pyramids of number based on your food chains.

Pyramids of biomass

Pyramids of number do not always look like pyramids. For example the food chain:

Oak tree → caterpillars → blue tits

Forms a 'pyramid' like this:

Don't be put off, always put the producer at the bottom and arrange the other feeding levels (called **trophic** levels) above it in the order in which they appear in a food chain.

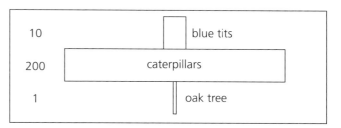

A more accurate way to show what is happening is by a **pyramid of biomass**. This shows the mass of the organisms feeding at that level, rather than the number. A pyramid of biomass for the food chain above would be:

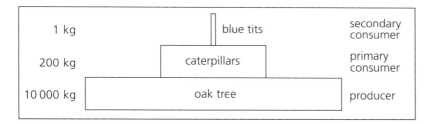

A pyramid of biomass shows the amount of energy moving along the food chain and that less energy passes on from level to level. This is because only some of the energy which organisms use is stored in their bodies. The rest is:

• used for life processes like movement, respiration and keeping warm
• wasted in faeces (undigested food).

This means that an area of land can feed more people with plant food than if it is used for producing meat for people, because meat adds another level into the pyramid.

Food webs

A **food web** is made up of many food chains and gives a more accurate picture of feeding relationships because very few animals only eat one type of food. For example, it is unlikely that blue tits only eat caterpillars.

Now do this

2 Which trophic level do sheep feed at?

3 What is the main difference between a food chain and a food web?

Cycling and decay

What happens to all the waste and dead animals and plants produced in an ecosystem?

They are used for food by living things called **decomposers**. Decomposers are very important because materials need to be broken down (**decay**) so that the nutrients they contain can be used again by other living things.

Living things are mostly made up of carbohydrates and proteins. Both of these contain carbon, hydrogen and oxygen. Proteins contain nitrogen as well. These are called **organic** compounds and all their elements are recycled to form new life.

An example of this recycling can be seen in the **carbon cycle**.

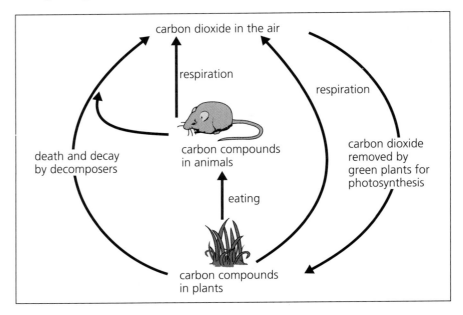

In the carbon cycle:
- decomposers (**bacteria** and **fungi**) in the soil release carbon dioxide into the air as they respire
- plants and animals release carbon dioxide into the air as they respire
- plants use carbon dioxide from the air to make carbohydrates and proteins
- animals get their carbohydrates by eating plants
- animals and plants die and decomposers feed on them, and so on.

Decomposers in the soil also release minerals and heat energy to the soil around them. They help to keep the soil warm!

Now do this

1. What is a decomposer?
2. Name **two** groups of living things which can act as decomposers.
3. Why are decomposers so important?

More carbon for the cycle

There are other parts of the carbon cycle as well. If decomposed materials cannot be recycled by other living things they may form fossil fuels. For example coal and oil were formed millions of years ago from dead organisms trapped beneath mud or rock.

As these fuels contain a lot of carbon from living things, burning them releases carbon dioxide into the air. Burning any material which was once a plant or animal (like wood, paper, animal tissues) releases carbon dioxide.

Air pollution

As the human population gets bigger and bigger, more and more fossil fuels are burnt in cars, factories and houses. This releases a great deal of carbon dioxide into the air.

At the same time, humans are cutting down trees to make more land to use. A lot of tropical rainforest has been cut down to make land for farming. This means that there are fewer trees to take up the extra carbon dioxide by photosynthesis. Sometimes trees are burned which leads to even more carbon dioxide in the air. More carbon dioxide in the atmosphere upsets the balance of the carbon cycle.

More carbon dioxide in the Earth's atmosphere makes the Earth warmer. This is called the **greenhouse effect**. It may melt some of the polar ice which would raise sea levels and flood many low lying habitats.

Burning fossil fuels causes other pollution in the air because they produce sulphur dioxide on burning. This dissolves in rainwater making it acid. When this **acid rain** falls on plants it can kill them. It also falls into lakes and can kill the life there.

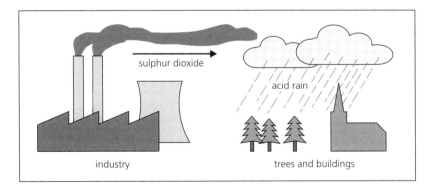
sulphur dioxide

acid rain

industry   trees and buildings

Now do this

4 Describe **two** problems caused by burning fossil fuels.

5 What would you add to the carbon cycle on the opposite page?

Reproduction

When plants and animals **reproduce** they make new plants and animals (offspring) like themselves. There are two main ways of reproducing.

Asexual reproduction

In asexual reproduction, one parent produces offspring which are identical to the parent. For example, spider plants and strawberries both grow runners with new plants on them.

Potatoes reproduce asexually by producing tubers and tulips by producing bulbs.

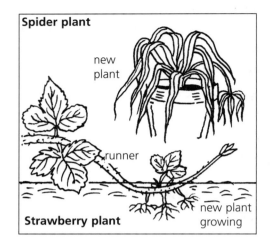

Spider plant

new plant

runner

Strawberry plant

new plant growing

The new plants that are produced asexually are produced by cells in the parents dividing by **mitosis**. They are called **clones**, which means identical to the parent. When we take **cuttings** of plants to grow we are producing clones.

Sexual reproduction

Sexual reproduction involves two parents which produce male and female sex cells called **gametes**. This is why it is called sexual reproduction.

In animals, the male gametes are called **sperm** and female gametes are called **eggs**. During sexual reproduction the sperm and egg join together at **fertilisation** to form a **zygote**. This develops into an embryo and then, in humans, into a baby.

Sperm comes from the male sex organs. Eggs come from the female sex organs.

The result of sexual reproduction is offspring who are unique individuals but also similar to their parents. This is because they have a mix of characteristics from both parents. How are these characteristics passed on?

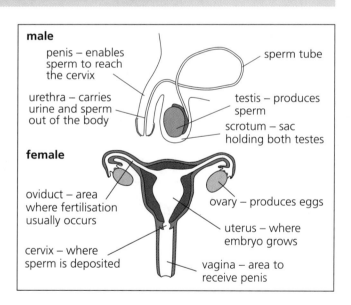

male

penis – enables sperm to reach the cervix

sperm tube

urethra – carries urine and sperm out of the body

testis – produces sperm

scrotum – sac holding both testes

female

oviduct – area where fertilisation usually occurs

ovary – produces eggs

uterus – where embryo grows

cervix – where sperm is deposited

vagina – area to receive penis

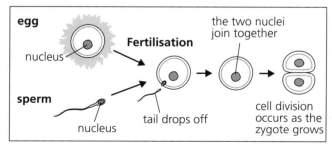

egg

nucleus

Fertilisation

the two nuclei join together

sperm

nucleus

tail drops off

cell division occurs as the zygote grows

Now do this

1   Why do you think reproduction by one parent only is called asexual?

2   What is a gamete?

3   Name the two gametes produced by humans.

Chromosomes

The nucleus of every cell has **chromosomes**. These carry all the information about our characteristics. Every chromosome carries thousands of **genes** and each gene helps to control the way our bodies are formed. For example, one set of genes controls eye colour, another hair colour and so on. Some of each parent's genes are passed on to the offspring.

Chromosomes are long molecules of DNA.

Most body cells have the same number of chromosomes. Each species of plant or animal has a different number of chromosomes. Human body cells have 46, arranged in 23 pairs.

Gametes are different. They contain only **half** of each pair of chromosomes normally found in body cells. When male and female gametes fuse at fertilisation the zygote then has a full set.

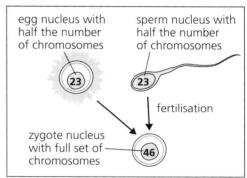

Deciding a baby's sex

Your chromosomes also control which sex you are. One pair is called the sex pair. There are two types of sex chromosome, the **X chromosome** and the **Y chromosome**.

Gametes have either an X chromosome or a Y chromosome. If two gametes which both have an X chromosome fuse the offspring is female (**XX**). If a gamete carrying an X and one carrying a Y fuse the offspring is male (**XY**).

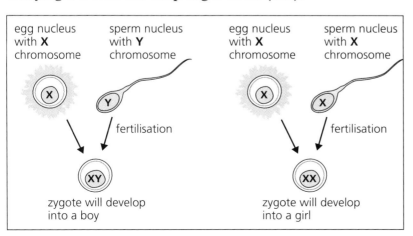

Now do this

4   The egg always carries an X chromosome. Why?

5   A cat cell has 38 chromosomes. How many do its gametes have?

Variation

Most of your characteristics depend on the information in the genes received from your parents. They depend on which of your parents' genes were carried by the gametes which formed you. So you may have similar characteristics to your parents, but in different combinations.

These differences between parents and offspring and between people in a population are called **variation**.

Mutations

Sometimes there are changes (**mutations**) to genes or to chromosomes and this may affect the characteristics of the individuals who inherit these genes or chromosomes. For example, some human eggs have 24 not 23 chromosomes and this gives rise to Down's syndrome in offspring formed from the egg.

Other mutations can be caused by:

- chromosomes not being copied correctly in cells
- exposure to radiation
- exposure to certain chemicals.

Genetic diseases

Some diseases are caused by faulty genes inherited from the parents. Examples are: sickle cell anaemia, cystic fibrosis, muscular dystrophy and haemophilia.

 Now do this

1   What is a mutation?
2   Give three possible causes of mutation.
3   Give an example of a chromosome mutation.

Lookalikes

Sometimes two individuals do have identical genes. Identical twins are formed from the same single fertilised egg which divides after fertilisation. Non-identical twins do not have an identical genetic make-up. They are produced from two eggs released from the ovaries at the same time but which are fertilised separately.

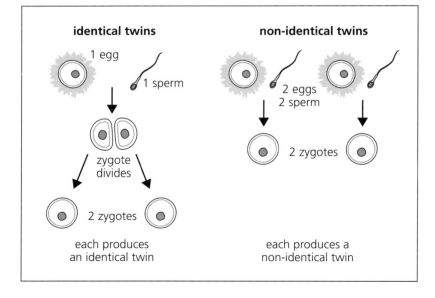

identical twins

1 egg
1 sperm

zygote divides

2 zygotes

each produces an identical twin

non-identical twins

2 eggs
2 sperm

2 zygotes

each produces a non-identical twin

Discontinuous variation is when you either have a characteristic or you do not have it. It is controlled by genes, for example eye colour, blood group.

Continuous variation is when there is a range of differences in one characteristic, for example height. It is controlled largely by the environment.

Selective breeding

We take advantage of variation when we **selectively breed** plants and animals. This involves picking individuals with the characteristics we want and breeding them. The best offspring are selected and bred. This is repeated over many generations.

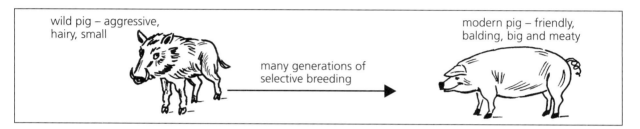

wild pig – aggressive, hairy, small

many generations of selective breeding

modern pig – friendly, balding, big and meaty

The table shows some of the reasons why we selectively breed.

Desired characteristic	Example
attractive appearance	dogs and cats
non-aggressive behaviour	domesticated animals
good milk production	cows
disease resistance	strawberries
high yield	wheat
flavour	tomatoes

Now do this

4 a What characteristic would you want to breed into racehorses?

b How would you do it?

Environmental variation

Most of your characteristics are influenced by genes but some are also affected by your environment. For example, your genes may make you tall, but if you are well fed as a child you may be even taller. A child's weight at birth is partly determined by genes but partly by its mother's health and age.

Very hot sun can make fair skin brown and brown hair fair. And you can change your hair colour and shape with chemicals any time you like!

Plants are also affected by their environment. For example, wind can affect the shape of a tree.

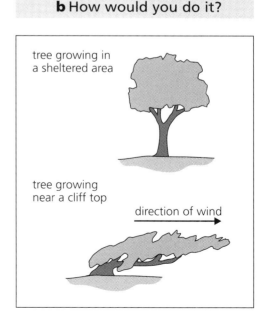

tree growing in a sheltered area

tree growing near a cliff top

direction of wind

Fossils and evolution

Animals and plants have gradually developed (**evolved**) from much simpler forms over many millions of years. This process is called **evolution** and **fossils** provide evidence for it.

Fossils are the remains of dead organisms which have become preserved in rock.

Organism dies by the water's edge.

Water level rises and dead organism gradually becomes covered in mud.

The soft parts decay but the hard bits (bone and cellulose) survive long enough to absorb minerals from the water.

As layers of sediment build up on top of the fossil it becomes embedded in a layer of sedimentary rock.

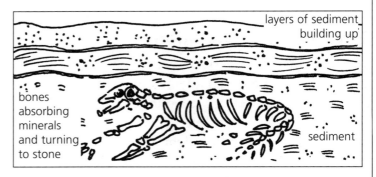

Now do this

Look at the formation of a fossil above and cover the labels on the left.

1 Now look at the pictures and describe in your own words how a fossil is formed.

Evolution

Fossils show that the modern horse has evolved from a much smaller animal which lived in marsh lands 60 million years ago.

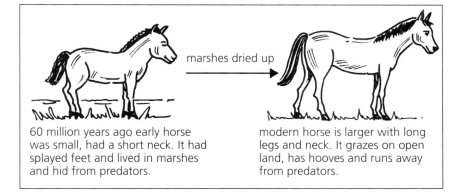

marshes dried up

60 million years ago early horse was small, had a short neck. It had splayed feet and lived in marshes and hid from predators.

modern horse is larger with long legs and neck. It grazes on open land, has hooves and runs away from predators.

What can fossils tell us?

The fossil record shows that the variety of living things around today did not appear all at once many years ago. Gradually over the years as new organisms have evolved, other organisms have died out.

Dinosaurs lived up until 65 million years ago, but we only know about them from the fossil evidence. We are relative newcomers to the world with our earliest ancestors making an appearance only 6 million years ago.

However, the record of evolution we have from fossils is incomplete for a variety of reasons:

- some body parts may not have fossilised
- fossilisation was a comparatively rare event
- we have not yet discovered all the fossils in the rocks of the world (many of which are buried deep underground).

This means that the fossil records are open to different interpretations. According to some religious groups, all living things were created at the same time. Therefore dinosaurs and man were created together – but we just have not found the fossil evidence yet!

Now do this

2 What is a fossil?

3 What sort of rocks are fossils most likely to be found in?

4 Explain why the modern horse has changed so much from its ancestor 60 million years ago.

5 Give **two** reasons why the fossil record is incomplete.

The working plant

The parts of a plant

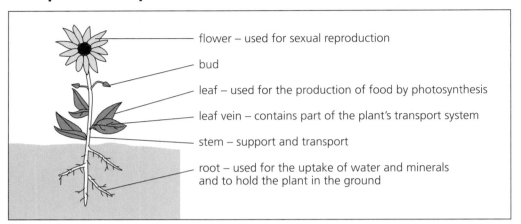

flower – used for sexual reproduction

bud

leaf – used for the production of food by photosynthesis

leaf vein – contains part of the plant's transport system

stem – support and transport

root – used for the uptake of water and minerals and to hold the plant in the ground

How do plants produce their food?

Plants make their own food by **photosynthesis**, using water, light and carbon dioxide.

Carbon dioxide and water are **needed** for photosynthesis, therefore they are the **reactants**. Plants use the hydrogen in the water to make glucose.

Glucose and oxygen are **produced** by photosynthesis, therefore they are the **products**. Oxygen is a waste product

sunlight absorbed by chlorophyll in the plant's leaf

energy in the sunlight used to drive the photosynthesis reaction

water comes in through root hair cells

carbon dioxide comes in from the air

oxygen out

Photosynthesis can be written as a **word equation**.

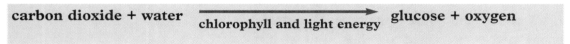

carbon dioxide + water $\xrightarrow{\text{chlorophyll and light energy}}$ glucose + oxygen

Green plants do not eat, they photosynthesis.

Now do this

1   Explain how green plants make their food.

2   Write out the word equation for photosynthesis.

3   Where does the carbon dioxide for photosynthesis come from?

4   Where does the water for photosynthesis come from?

What makes plants photosynthesise faster?

- more carbon dioxide because carbon dioxide is one of the reactants of photosynthesis
- more light because the energy of the light is used to drive the photosynthesis reaction
- higher temperatures

So a hot, sunny day will allow a plant to photosynthesise more quickly than a cold, dull day. This is why plants grow faster in the summer.

Where do plants make their food?

Plants make their food in the leaves which are:

- **broad** to catch as much sunlight as possible
- **thin** to allow light to reach all the cells easily
- **full of chlorophyll** to trap light energy
- part of a **good transport system** (**veins**), and
- have **stomata** to allow gases in and out.

one stoma

lots of stomata

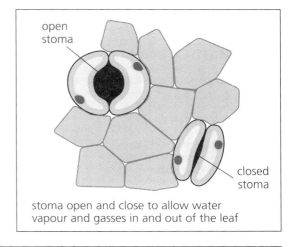

stoma open and close to allow water vapour and gasses in and out of the leaf

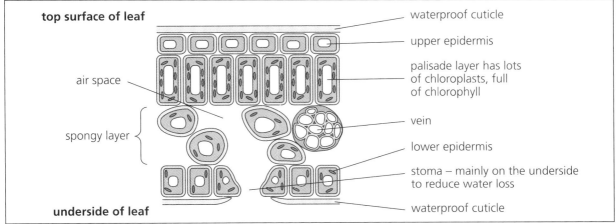

Now do this

5   Give **three** ways in which leaves are adapted for photosynthesis.

6   Name one substance which the plant can use which passes through stomata.

7   Do plants photosynthesise at night? Explain your answer.

Moving materials around the plant

Plants use food (glucose) produced during photosynthesis to make **all** the materials they need to live and grow.

Glucose may be:

- changed into sucrose to be transported around the plant
- changed into cellulose for new cell walls
- changed into proteins
- used to release energy (respiration)
- changed into large insoluble storage materials like starch.

So food needs to be moved around the plant to the growing or storage areas in the roots, shoots, flowers, fruits and buds.

Food on the move

The **phloem** carries dissolved food to the other parts of the plant. It is made of living cells. The phloem system covers all parts of the plant.

Water on the move

Plants need water in their leaves for photosynthesis. Water enters the plant through its **root hair** cells and travels up to the leaves in the **xylem**. The xylem forms long tubes throughout the plant. It is made up of dead cells with no cytoplasm (they look a bit like drinking straws).

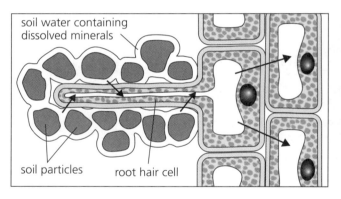

soil water containing dissolved minerals

soil particles   root hair cell

Root hair cells are good at taking up water because they are:

- long and thin therefore they have a large surface area, and
- have thin walls to help water to pass through.

Root hair cells also take up minerals dissolved in the water.

Nitrogen, phosphorus and potassium are the main plant minerals, together with small amounts of magnesium which is needed to make chlorophyll. All of these are needed for healthy plant growth. Fertilisers contain these minerals.

Now do this

1 Name the **two** transport systems in plants and state what each one is used for.

2 Suggest why plants which do not get enough magnesium look yellow and small.

3 List **three** uses of glucose in a plant.

Now do this

4 Explain what root hair cells do.

5 Complete all the labels on the diagram below.

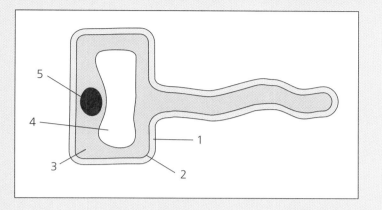

Xylem carries water and minerals.

Phloem carries food dissolved in water.

Diffusion

Diffusion is the movement of particles from an area where there are lots of them (high concentration) to an area where there are very few of them (a low concentration).

Once in the root hair cell the water and dissolved minerals diffuse across the root to the xylem.

Now do this

Look at cells A and B.

Key

  water particles

6 Which cell, A or B would lose water by diffusion?

7 Explain your answer.

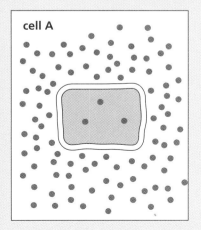

cell A

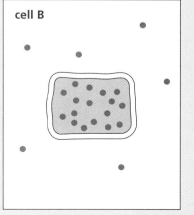

cell B

Tracking the xylem and phloem

Going up!

The xylem transports water and dissolved minerals from the roots to the leaves. They are 'sucked' up the xylem by **transpiration**.

Transpiration is the evaporation of water from inside the leaves to the surrounding air.

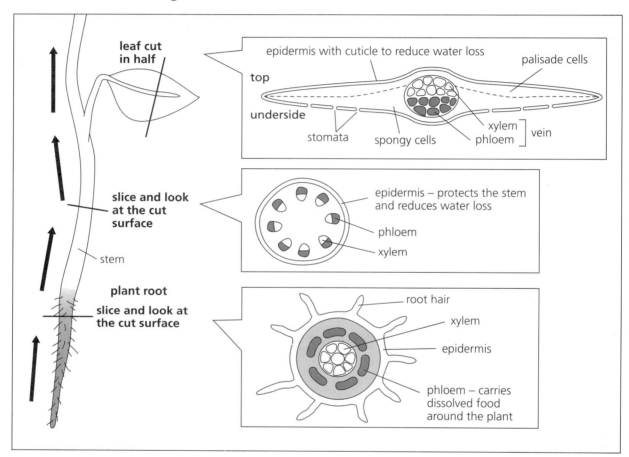

The water vapour passes out of the leaves by diffusion:

- water diffuses from the xylem into the spongy cells
- water evaporates into the air space
- water vapour diffuses out of the stomata
- water lost from the spongy cells is replaced by more water from the xylem.

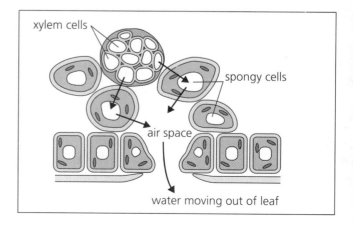

Now do this

1 a Explain why a piece of celery gradually turns blue when it is stood in a beaker of blue ink for a week.

b Complete the diagram of the cross section of the celery stem to show what it would look like at the end of the week.

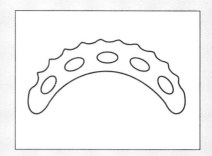

Transpiration

Transpiration provides water for:

- photosynthesis
- cooling the plant (it is the plant's version of sweating)
- movement of minerals
- support.

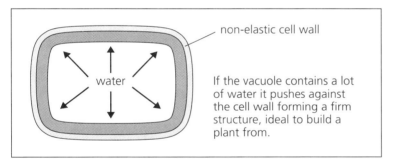

non-elastic cell wall

If the vacuole contains a lot of water it pushes against the cell wall forming a firm structure, ideal to build a plant from.

water

Factors affecting the speed of transpiration

Transpiration is increased by:
- more light because water is used up as the plant photosynthesises more
- increased temperatures because photosynthesis and evaporation increase with temperature
- increased air movement, which increases evaporation
- decreased humidity as water evaporates more easily into dry air.

Now do this

2 Stomata are mainly on the underside of a leaf. Why do you think this is?

3 What is transpiration?

4 Give **three** reasons why transpiration is so important for plants.

5 How does: **a** the carbon dioxide needed for photosynthesis get into a leaf; **b** the oxygen produced during photosynthesis leave the plant?

Respiration – releasing energy

Your body needs energy just to stay alive!

Energy is released from sugar (glucose) when it reacts with oxygen in our cells.
This is called **aerobic respiration**.

It happens in *all* of our cells *all* of the time.
Aerobic respiration can be written as a **word** equation.

glucose + oxygen → carbon dioxide + water + ENERGY

Taking exercise

Working your muscles needs energy. So the more we exercise the more energy we need. The body copes by:

- breathing rate increasing to bring more oxygen into the body
- pulse rate increasing to speed up blood flow around the body – the blood carries oxygen and glucose to the respiring cells
- increasing aerobic respiration in the muscle cells.

Running out of oxygen

During vigorous exercise the body cannot get enough oxygen, so the cells have to respire **anaerobically**. (This means without oxygen.)

Anaerobic respiration releases energy but not as much as aerobic respiration does. It also produces a mild poison, lactic acid.

Anaerobic respiration can be written as a word equation.

glucose → lactic acid + some ENERGY

Breathing out

One of the waste products of respiration is carbon dioxide. It is important to remove this from the blood because it is toxic. Carbon dioxide is carried to the lungs by the blood. Then it is removed from the body by the lungs when we breath out. The exhaled air contains more carbon dioxide, less oxygen and more moisture than inhaled air.

Plant cells also **respire** all the time to release energy.

Your body is like the engine in a car. The petrol is the food. It is burnt in oxygen to release energy to run the car.

Different foods contain different amounts of energy. Carbohydrates and fats provide lots of energy. Vegetables and fruit provide far less energy.

Now do this

1 Unscramble the following letters to make six words associated with respiration.

cctlai   xgoeny

ygnree   bcoaaenri

bcaeior   csgeoul

Respiration is the release of _____ from foods such as _____ . If there is a plentiful supply of _____ then the cells will use _____ respiration. However if there is insufficient oxygen available then the cells may use _____ respiration in which case they will produce _____ acid and less energy.

Now use the words to fill in the gaps in the passage above:

2 Write word equations for **a** aerobic respiration and **b** anaerobic respiration.

3 Where does respiration take place?

4 Give two ways in which the body copes with increased exercise.

Plants can respire anaerobically but when they do, they produce alcohol (ethanol) and carbon dioxide. This reaction is also called **fermentation**.

Fermentation can be written as a word equation.

glucose → ethanol + carbon dioxide + some ENERGY

Fermentation is used in breadmaking and brewing. In breadmaking the carbon dioxide makes the bread light and airy, and in brewing the useful product is the ethanol which gives the beers and wines their alcoholic content.

Keeping a balance

The rate at which oxygen is taken into the body is a measure of how fast the body is using it up. That is, it is a measure of the **metabolic rate** of the body.

Different foods contain different amounts of energy therefore care must be taken that the energy intake is enough for the energy needs of the body. Otherwise there will be an increase or decrease in body mass.

energy intake	energy requirement

Now do this

5 What is fermentation?

6 Write a word equation for fermentation.

7 Explain why fermentation is used to produce **one** named product.

Homeostasis

Homeostasis literally means 'keeping things the same'. Your body works to keep conditions just right for your cells to work well and this process is called **homeostasis**.

What needs controlling?

The things which need controlling in the blood are:

- glucose concentration
- water and salt concentration
- carbon dioxide level
- temperature
- waste products in the blood, such as urea.

The water balance

If the balance of water in our bodies is upset we either **dehydrate** (dry out), or swell up with excess fluid. We cannot survive either extreme for long.

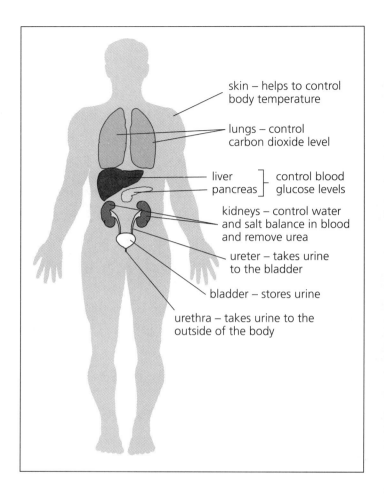

skin – helps to control body temperature

lungs – control carbon dioxide level

liver
pancreas } control blood glucose levels

kidneys – control water and salt balance in blood and remove urea

ureter – takes urine to the bladder

bladder – stores urine

urethra – takes urine to the outside of the body

**food and drink
(water in)**

**urine, sweat and breath
(water out)**

Now do this

1   What does homeostasis mean?
2   Which two body organs are used to control blood glucose level?
3   Name three substances filtered out of the blood in the kidney.
4   What is passed out of the bladder down the urethra?
5   Where does carbon dioxide leave the body?

Controlling body temperature

When our cells respire, some of the energy released is **heat** energy. We use this to keep us warm.

Think about what you do when you feel cold. You might stamp your feet or rub your hands together, or even shiver. All of these actions involve respiration which releases energy and this warms you up!

If the blood temperature goes above 37 °C the brain notices and switches on **cooling mechanisms** to reduce the temperature. If the blood temperature goes below 37 °C the brain switches on **warming mechanisms**.

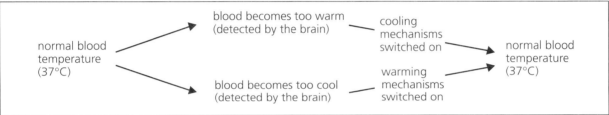

The mechanisms

Cooling mechanisms	Warming mechanisms
sweating – heat from the body used to evaporate sweat from the skin surface	shivering – muscles make heat by respiration to warm us up
vasodilation – blood vessels near skin surface open to allow blood to flow near to the surface of the body and lose heat by radiation to the air	vasoconstriction – blood vessels running near skin surface close, diverting the blood back to the warmer parts of the body
behavioural – take some clothes off	behavioural – put some extra clothes on

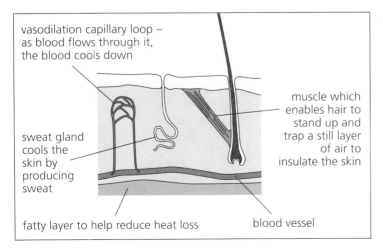

vasodilation capillary loop – as blood flows through it, the blood cools down

muscle which enables hair to stand up and trap a still layer of air to insulate the skin

sweat gland cools the skin by producing sweat

fatty layer to help reduce heat loss

blood vessel

 Now do this

6 Which part of the body checks the temperature of the blood?

7 Explain how sweating helps cool us down.

8 Give **two** ways in which the body warms itself up.

Keeping healthy

Your body has to defend itself against microbes which can attack it and cause disease.

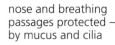

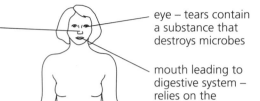

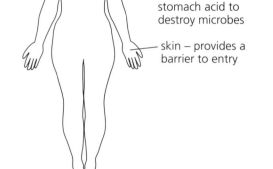

Fighting back

If the skin is damaged, blood forms a second line of defence by:

- forming a clot and scab to block entry to microbes
- allowing white blood cells to escape from blood vessels to attack any invading microbes.

There are two types of white blood cell. One type 'eats' the microbes.

Another word for microbes and other foreign materials in your body is **antigen**.

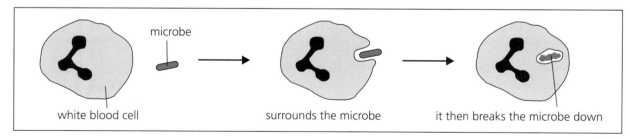

white blood cell · surrounds the microbe · it then breaks the microbe down

The other type produces chemicals called **antibodies** which attack the microbes and destroy them.

The white blood cell makes contact with the microbe and identifies it. It then divides to produce a lot more white blood cells all capable of releasing the right antibody when they recognise the same microbe.

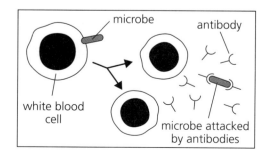

Now do this

1 How are the eyes protected from microbe invasion?
2 If the skin is damaged, how does the body continue to protect itself?
3 What is an antibody?
4 Why is it important that white blood cells can escape from blood vessels?

Immunity

Once your body has met a microbe and made antibodies against it, it does not forget. When you meet the same type of microbe, your body is waiting. It quickly produces lots of antibodies so you are unlikely to get the disease again. This is called **immunity**. Unfortunately it does not work very well with colds and flu, because there are so many different strains of them. Antibodies to one cold strain will not give you immunity to any of the other strains!

Treatment

If you do become ill, you may need medicine to make you feel better. Medicines contain **drugs**. A **drug** is a substance that changes the way in which your body works. When taken as painkillers or antibiotics they can be very useful.

Problems with drugs

Some drugs are **addictive**. This means that the person taking the drug becomes dependent on the drug. They then have to keep taking the drug.

A **stimulant** drug speeds up brain activity; a **depressant** drug slows down brain activity.

Drug	Action	Negative effects
caffeine	stimulant	can cause sleeplessness
nicotine	anaesthetic	can stop cilia in trachea beating, leading to a build up of mucus and a smokers' cough
alcohol	depressant	may slow down brain activity to the point of passing out; reduces ability to make judgements; prolonged use may result in damage to the brain; it poisons the liver leading to liver damage
solvents	depressants	may slow down brain activity to the point where you die

Some drugs produce **withdrawal symptoms** if the user stops or is prevented from taking the drug. These vary in severity from a headache if you are deprived of coffee for the day, to sickness, blinding headaches and an inability to sleep, eat or do anything.

Analgesics are painkillers which depress the brain's activity.

Now do this

5 Explain why smoking may make someone more likely to get lung infections.
6 What is a drug?
7 What is the difference between a depressant and a stimulant? Give an example of each.

Concept map

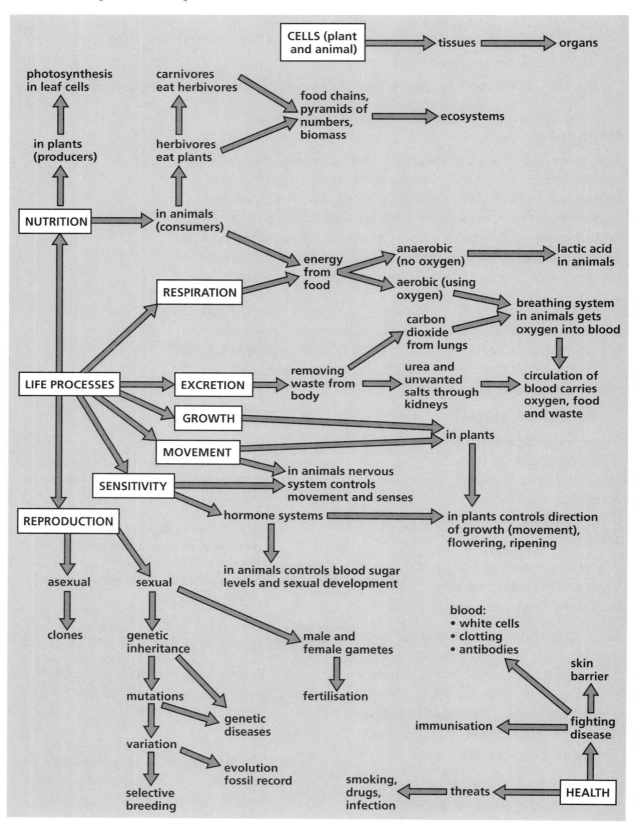

Exam questions

1 The figure shows several different types of cell.

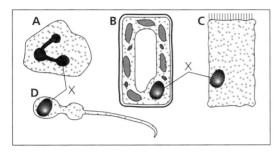

a What is the name of structure **X** in all of the cells? [1]

b State **one** reason why **X** is needed in a cell. [1]

c Which **one** of these cells is from a plant? Give a reason for your answer. [2]

[**4 marks**]

2 The figure shows a human thorax.

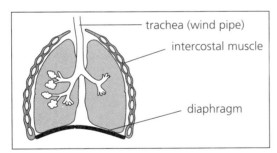

a Explain what each labelled part does. [3]

b Inside the lungs are alveoli. This is where gas exchange occurs.

i Name the process by which the gases move through the alveoli [1]

ii List **three** features of alveoli which adapt them for gas exchange. [3]

[**7 marks**]

3 The small intestine is lined with villi to absorb digested food.

a What is digestion? [2]

b Complete the sentences
Proteins are broken down into
_____. [1]
Starch is broken down into
_____. [1]
Fats are broken down into _____
_____ and _____. [2]

c List **two** features of villi which adapt them for absorbing digested food. [2]

[**8 marks**]

4 The figure shows two sets of apparatus which are kept at the same temperature throughout the experiment. Flask **A** contains some maggots and flask **B** does not. Soda lime is a chemical which absorbs

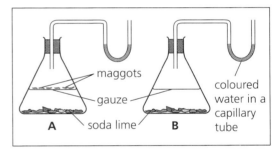

carbon dioxide.

a Suggest how both sets of apparatus could be kept at the same temperature throughout the experiment. [1]

b Name the process taking place in flask **A** but not in flask **B**. [1]

c Describe and explain what will happen to the coloured water in each set of apparatus during the experiment. [3]

[**5 marks**]

5 The figure shows a plant.

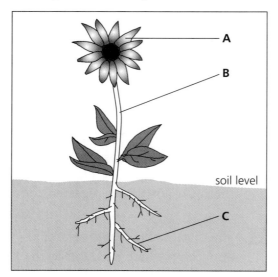

a Explain what each of the labelled parts **A**, **B** and **C** do. [3]

b The leaf of a plant is used for photosynthesis.

  i Complete the following word equation to show what happens during photosynthesis:

  carbon dioxide + _____ →
  glucose + _____ [2]

  ii How does carbon dioxide enter a leaf for photosynthesis? [2]

  iii Give **three** uses of the glucose produced by photosynthesis. [3]

  iv Explain why plants photosynthesise more rapidly on a hot, sunny day than on a dull, cold day. [2]
  [12 marks]

6 The figure shows an experiment set up using four leaves.

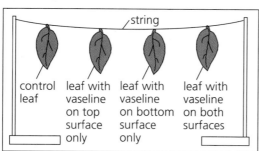

Each leaf was treated, weighed and the mass recorded **before** attaching to the string. After 36 hours each leaf was reweighed and the change in mass calculated. The table shows the results.

Leaf	Starting mass (g)	Ending mass (g)	Change in mass (g)
control	25.2	22.9	lost 2.3
vaseline on top	24.1	22.3	
vaseline on bottom	25.0	24.7	
vaseline on both top and bottom	23.5	23.5	

a Complete the table. [3]

b What is being lost from the leaves? [1]

c Suggest an explanation for the difference in the results. [2]
[6 marks]

7 The figure shows a cross section through a plant stem.

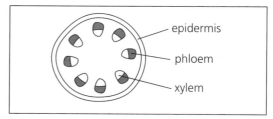

a Explain what each labelled part does. [3]

b Name the process which causes water to move through a plant. [1]

c State **two** uses of water in a plant. [2]
[6 marks]

8 The figure shows a cross section of an eye.

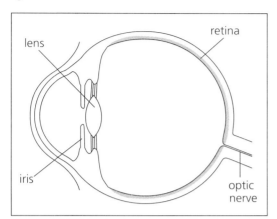

Explain what each labelled part does. [4]

[**4 marks**]

9 The figure shows a section of a human heart.

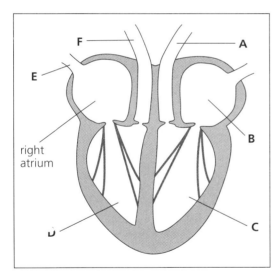

a Name the chamber labelled **D**. [1]

b Which labelled blood vessel contains oxygenated blood? [1]

c State whether the blood in each of the vessels **E** and **F** is flowing towards the heart or away from the heart. [2]

d What is the function of the valve between chambers **B** and **C**? [2]

e What tissue is the heart made of? [1]

[**7 marks**]

10 The figure shows how we control our body temperature.

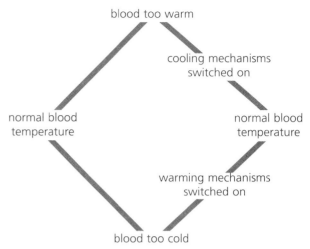

a Draw an arrow head on the end of each line to show how temperature control is achieved. [2]

b Which part of the body detects changes in the blood temperature? [1]

c Describe **two** mechanisms the body uses to help it cool down. [4]

[**7 marks**]

11 The figure shows part of a field food web.

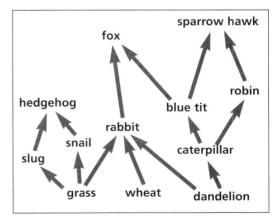

The questions refer to the food web.

ai Write down a food chain with **four** different organisms which forms part of this food web. [2]

ii Name **one** predator in the food web. [1]

iii Name **one** producer in the food web. [1]

iv Name **two** carnivores in the food web. [2]

b The farmer uses a selective weed killer on the field and the dandelions die. Explain what effect this might have on the sparrow hawks in the area. [2]

[8 marks]

12 The figure shows three pyramids of numbers.

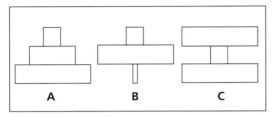

a Which pyramid of numbers describes a woodland with lots of squirrels and only a few foxes, **A**, **B** or **C**? [1]

b Which pyramid of numbers describes a flea ridden hedgehog living in a field. **A**, **B** or **C**? [1]

c Draw a pyramid of biomass in the space below, for a cabbage which is eaten by caterpillars which are then eaten by a blue tit. [2]

[4 marks]

13 Farmers can produce more food if they use herbicides, pesticides and fertilisers.

ai What are herbicides? [1]

ii What are pesticides? [1]

iii Explain why fertilisers enable plants to grow better. [2]

Look at the table. It shows the effect of increasing amounts of fertiliser on wheat yield.

Fertiliser (kg per m^2)	Wheat field (kg per m^2)
0.0	20
0.5	25
1.0	32
1.5	40
2.0	44
2.5	46
3.0	46

bi Draw a line graph on the grid provided. [3]

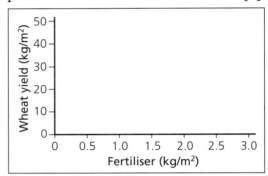

ii Use the graph to work out the most economical amount of fertiliser to add to your crop of wheat. Explain as fully as you can. [2]

iii Write **two** sentences to explain the problems of using fertilisers. [2]

[11 marks]

14 The figure shows the male reproductive system.

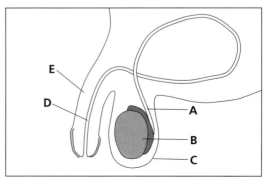

Name the parts labelled **A**, **B**, **C**, **D** and **E** and outline briefly what each does. [10]

[10 marks]

15 The figure shows a human sperm cell.

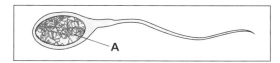

a What is part **A**? [1]

Inside part **A** are lots of chromosomes.

b What is the function of the chromosomes? [1]

In a human liver cell there are 46 chromosomes.

c How many are there in a human sperm cell? [1]

d Some people have a condition called Down's syndrome. How are their chromosomes different from those of people who do not have Down's syndrome? [1]

The sex chromosomes in humans are **X** and **Y**.

e What combination of sex chromosomes does a male contain? [1]
[**5 marks**]

16 Dog breeders have used selective breeding for many years to produce puppies with the required appearance and temperament. Farmers also use animals and plants which have been selectively bred.

a Suggest **two** features that a farmer might wish to breed into a farm animal. [2]

b Suggest **two** features that a farmer might wish to breed into a crop plant. [2]
[**4 marks**]

17 The figure shows a sperm cell and an egg cell joining.

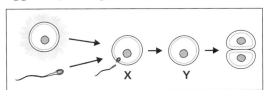

a What is the name given to the process shown at **X** in the figure? [1]

b What is the new cell (**Y**) called? [1]

c Whereabouts in the female reproductive system does **X** normally occur? [1]

d What normally happens to **Y** in the female reproductive system? [1]
[**4 marks**]

18 This key can be used to identify some common animals.

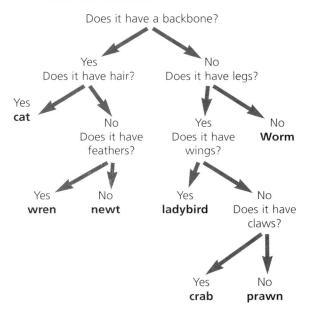

a Use the key to describe **three** characteristics of the crab. [3]

b Which other animal shown in this key is most like the crab? [1]
[**4 marks**]

19 The figure shows an eagle.

a Look at the figure and describe **three** features of the eagle which make it a successful predator. [3]

Eagles often eat small animals such as rabbits. In order to survive rabbits have certain adaptations to help them avoid predators.

b Suggest **two** ways in which rabbits are adapted to avoid predators. [2]

[5 marks]

20 The table shows the sulphur dioxide released into the atmosphere in the United Kingdom over a period of 40 years.

Year	Sulphur dioxide released in the United Kingdom (in million tonnes)
1950	4.6
1960	5.8
1970	6.0
1980	5.2
1990	4.9

a Use the information in the table to complete the graph below. [2]

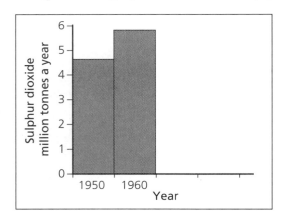

b Suggest an explanation for the shape of the graph. [1]

c Sulphur dioxide pollution causes acid rain. Write **two** sentences to describe the harmful effects of acid rain. [2]

[5 marks]

21 The table shows the concentration of alcohol in the blood of a person who has been drinking.

Time	5 pm	6 pm	7 pm	8 pm	9 pm	10 pm	11 pm
alcohol (mg per 100 cm^3 blood)	70	100	210	180	140	90	50

a Use the information in the table to complete the line graph. [3]

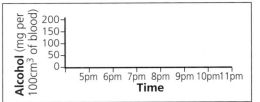

b Give **one** reason why it is unsafe to drive with alcohol in your blood. [1]

c Long-term alcohol abuse can seriously damage your health. Explain **two** ways in which alcohol may do this. [2]

d Alcohol is a drug used by many.
 i What is meant by the word drug? [1]
 ii Name **two** other drugs. [2]

[9 marks]

22 Look at the table. It shows the energy value of certain foods.

Food	Energy (kJ in 100 g food)
bacon	940
baked beans	270
mashed potatoes	340
pasta	1400
sausages	1200

a Which **two** foods have the most energy? [2]

b Simon had sausage (200 g), bacon (100 g) and baked beans (150 g) for beakfast. Calculate how much energy his breakfast contained. [2]

[4 marks]

AT3

Materials and their Properties

Solids, liquids and gases

Everything is made of very small particles which are too small to see. The particles are always moving; the hotter they are the more they move. Particles are arranged in different ways in solids, liquids and gases.

Solids

The particles in a solid are close together. The particles stay in the same places, so solids keep their shape – even though the particles vibrate more as the solid gets hotter. You can't move the particles any closer, so solids can't be compressed into a smaller space.

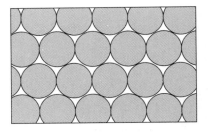

Liquids

In a liquid the particles are usually **slightly** further apart than in a solid. They can now move about, so liquids do not have a fixed shape. You still can't move the particles any closer so liquids can't be compressed into a smaller space. As a liquid gets hotter, the particles move faster. If they move fast enough the liquid boils and the particles break away. They become a gas.

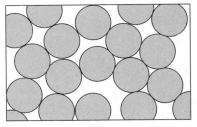

Gases

In a gas, the particles are **very** far apart. This means that gases have no shape and it is easy to compress them into a small space. The particles move very fast.

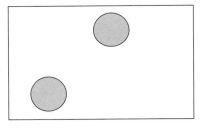

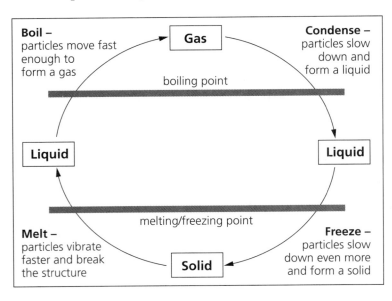

Remember that in solids the particles move in a different way.

Remember to draw gas particles really far apart.

Now do this

1   Give **two** ways in which liquid particles are similar to gas particles.

2   Why are solids hard?

Elements, compounds and mixtures

Atoms, molecules and elements

The particles inside everything are made of **atoms**. Some particles are just single atoms on their own. Sometimes groups of atoms bond together to make **molecules**. There are 104 different types of atom. Each different type of atom is a different **element**. Some common elements are hydrogen, carbon, oxygen, sulphur, iron.

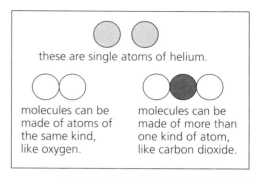

these are single atoms of helium.

molecules can be made of atoms of the same kind, like oxygen.

molecules can be made of more than one kind of atom, like carbon dioxide.

Compounds

Atoms of different elements can join together to make **compounds**. Compounds are always made from atoms of more than one element, for example, carbon dioxide.

carbon dioxide is a compound made of **two** types of atom

Compounds are nothing like the elements that are inside them. For example, sodium chloride is the salt that you sprinkle on your chips. It is made from two elements that have joined together, sodium (a silvery metal) and chlorine (a poisonous gas). These elements on their own would kill you, yet you need the compound of the two to stay alive!

Mixtures

Some substances can be mixed together without joining up. When this happens they do not form compounds, they stay as **mixtures**. For example, air is a mixture of gases such as oxygen and nitrogen. Sea water is a mixture of water and salt – the salt is dissolved in the water but it does not form a compound with the water. Substances in a mixture do not join, so they are easy to separate out.

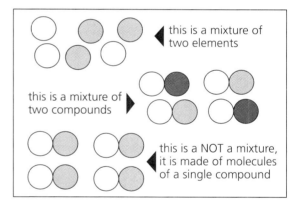

this is a mixture of two elements

this is a mixture of two compounds

this is a NOT a mixture, it is made of molecules of a single compound

Now do this

3   Which of the following are compounds:

hydrogen, hydrogen sulphide, oxygen, sugar, nitric acid, carbon?

4   Which of the following are mixtures:

salt and sand; sodium chloride; sugar; water; salty water?

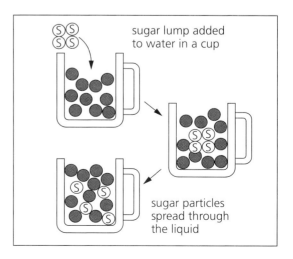

sugar lump added to water in a cup

sugar particles spread through the liquid

Separating mixtures

Substances in a mixture are not joined together, so you can separate them out again using one of these methods.

Filtration

If you have a liquid with an undissolved solid in it you can filter out the solid.

You can use filtration to get sand from a mixture of sand and salty water.

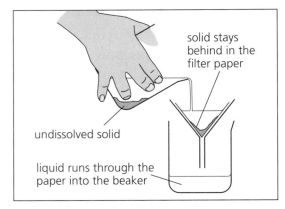

solid stays behind in the filter paper

undissolved solid

liquid runs through the paper into the beaker

Evaporation/crystallisation

You can use this method to get a solid from a solution. Gently heat the mixture so that the liquid evaporates into the air and the solid stays behind as crystals.

You can use evaporation and crystalisation to get salt out of salty water.

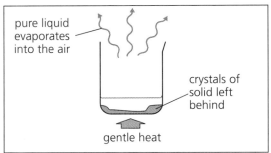

pure liquid evaporates into the air

crystals of solid left behind

gentle heat

Chromatography

You can use chromatography to see how many chemicals there are in a solution.

Put a drop of solution on a strip of filter paper and dip the end in water. As the water goes up the paper the chemicals separate and each moves a different distance up the paper.

You can use chromatography to see how many coloured dyes there are in black ink.

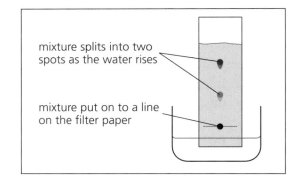

mixture splits into two spots as the water rises

mixture put on to a line on the filter paper

Now do this

1   Here are some separation problems. Some can be done by using just one of the methods in the table. Others will need more than one method. Copy the table and tick the methods that you need for each separation.

	Method		
	Dissolve	Filter	Evaporate
a to get solid salt out of salty water (like sea water)			
b to get sand from sand mixed with salty water			
c to get solid salt from sand mixed with salty water			
d to get solid salt from sand mixed with salt crystals			

Distillation

You can use **distillation** to get a pure liquid back out of a solution. You heat the solution in the flask. The liquid boils and turns into a gas. The gas goes through the condenser, and the cold surfaces inside the condenser turn the gas back into a liquid – it **condenses**. You can use this apparatus to get pure water from salty water.

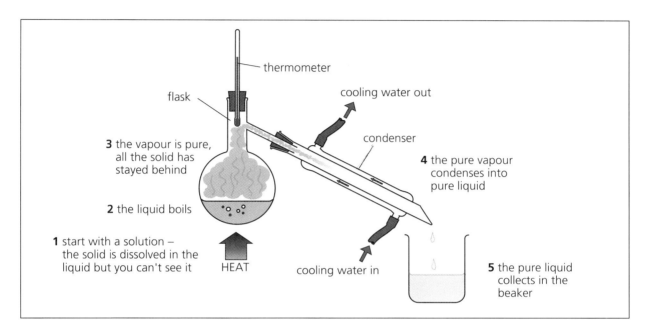

thermometer

flask

cooling water out

condenser

3 the vapour is pure, all the solid has stayed behind

4 the pure vapour condenses into pure liquid

2 the liquid boils

1 start with a solution – the solid is dissolved in the liquid but you can't see it

HEAT

cooling water in

5 the pure liquid collects in the beaker

Fractional distillation

If you distil several liquids mixed together in the normal way all the liquids will evaporate and you still have a mixture of liquids, not one pure liquid.

To separate them, you use the fact that the liquids have different boiling points. This is called **fractional distillation**. You can see how this works if you look at how crude oil is separated into different liquid hydrocarbons (page 58).

 Now do this

Red ink is made from a red powder dissolved in water.

2   If you boil red ink, what colour steam will you get?

3   If you distil red ink, what will end up in the beaker?

4   If you distil red ink, where is the powder at the end?

5   Alcohol is a liquid which mixes in with water. How can you separate them?

Chemical equations

Chemical reactions

When substances react chemically they turn into completely new substances. Sodium and chlorine turn into salt when they react. Hydrogen and oxygen turn into water. Salt is a compound of sodium and chlorine, water is a compound of hydrogen and oxygen. Chemical reactions are very difficult to undo.

Most chemical reactions either need heating to make them start or they give out heat as they happen. If you put iron filings into copper sulphate solution the solution gets warm – this is one sign that a chemical reaction has happened.

What is a chemical equation?

A chemical equation tells us what happens in a chemical reaction. It tells us what chemicals we start with (**reactants**) and what the chemicals turn into (**products**).

dangerous, silvery metal		choking green gas	salt, safe to eat
sodium	+	**chlorine** →	**sodium chloride**
REACTANT	+	**REACTANT** →	**PRODUCT**

In this reaction two chemicals have turned into one product chemical. All the atoms inside the two reactants are now inside the product chemical.

magnesium	+	**hydrochloric acid**	→	**magnesium chloride**	+	**hydrogen**
REACTANT	+	**REACTANT**	→	**PRODUCT**	+	**PRODUCT**

In this equation two reactant chemicals have turned into two product chemicals. All the atoms that made up the reactants are now inside the two product chemicals.

 Now do this

1 Copy out these equations and label each substance as either a reactant or a product:
   a hydrogen + oxygen → hydrogen oxide
   b carbon + iron oxide → carbon dioxide + iron
   c propane → hydrogen + propene

2 In a chemical reaction the reactants are sodium and water, the products are sodium hydroxide and hydrogen. Write this as a word equation.

Using symbols

It takes a long time to write out equations in words. It is a lot easier to write equations using symbols.

Each element has its own symbol. For example, carbon is C, oxygen is O. The formula for a substance made of several atoms shows the symbols for all its atoms. Carbon and oxygen make carbon dioxide, which is CO_2.

A word equation for the reaction looks like this:

carbon + oxygen → carbon dioxide

A symbol equation for the same reaction looks like this:

$$C + O_2 \rightarrow CO_2$$

Keep the equation on one line of the page. Don't let it go over on to a second line.

Balancing equations

All the atoms inside the reactant molecules end up inside the product molecules, so equations always have the same number of atoms on each side of the equation sign.

For example, hydrogen gas and chlorine gas will react with each other.

hydrogen + chlorine → hydrogen chloride

Hydrogen and chlorine molecules are made of pairs of atoms, so the symbol equation might look like this:

$$H_2 + Cl_2 \rightarrow HCl$$

But this means that there are two atoms of hydrogen and two of chlorine on the left but only one of each on the right. To balance this up we write

$$H_2 + Cl_2 \rightarrow 2HCl$$

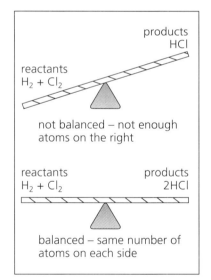

products
HCl

reactants
$H_2 + Cl_2$

not balanced – not enough atoms on the right

reactants
$H_2 + Cl_2$

products
2HCl

balanced – same number of atoms on each side

Now do this

3 Copy each equation, then for each one:
   Write down all the atoms of each element on the reactant side.
   Write down all the atoms of each element on the product side.

Does the equation balance?

a $Mg + Cl_2 \rightarrow MgCl_2$

b $Mg + O_2 \rightarrow 2MgO$

c $CH_4 + 2O_2 \rightarrow CO_2 + 2H_2O$

Rates of reaction

Chemical reactions happen at different speeds. You can see some of them around you. Rusting is a slow chemical reaction. Burning is a fast chemical reaction, explosions are even faster! The speed of a reaction is called its **rate**.

Speeding up reactions

Reactions happen when reactant particles collide and turn into products. The way to speed up most reactions is to make the particles collide more often.

1 Increase the **temperature**. This makes the reactant particles move faster so they hit each other more often. They also hit each other harder because they have more energy. Sodium thiosulphate solution ('thio') will go cloudy with dilute acid. If you warm the liquids the reaction will go faster.

look down here (wearing goggles)

thio and acid go cloudy

mark on paper disappears

2 Increase the **concentration**. This only works with a solution. Increasing concentration makes the particles get closer together, so they collide with the other reactant more often. 'Thio' goes cloudy more quickly when it is more concentrated.

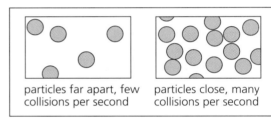

particles far apart, few collisions per second

particles close, many collisions per second

3 If one of the reactants is a solid, break it down into smaller lumps. This increases the **surface area**, there are then more places for the reaction to take place. Large marble chips react slowly with acid. If you use smaller marble chips with acid the reaction will go faster.

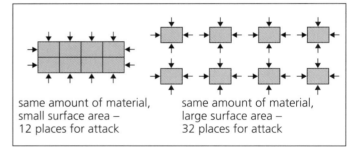

same amount of material, small surface area – 12 places for attack

same amount of material, large surface area – 32 places for attack

4 Use a **catalyst**. Catalysts speed up a reaction. They are only needed in small amounts and are not used up by the reaction, they can be re-used. Different reactions need different catalysts to speed them up. For example, hydrogen peroxide slowly breaks down into water and oxygen. To speed this up you can add manganese dioxide as a catalyst. All the manganese dioxide is left in the beaker at the end, and it can be used again.

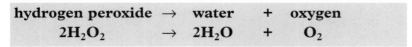

hydrogen peroxide $\rightarrow$ water + oxygen
$2H_2O_2$ $\rightarrow$ $2H_2O$ + O_2

Now do this

1 Give three ways of speeding up the reaction between acid solution and a solid carbonate.

2 Which ways will still work for a reaction between acid solution and a carbonate solution?

Measuring the speed (rate) of a reaction

How can you find the rate of a reaction? The easiest way is to measure how fast one of the products is made.

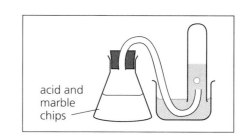

acid and marble chips

When marble chips react with acid you can measure the amount of carbon dioxide gas given off every minute. You can do this with a large syringe or by catching the gas in a test tube.

Reactions always start fast and then slow down as the reactant chemicals are used up.

Reactions carry on until one of the reactants runs out.

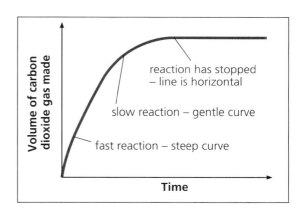

reaction has stopped – line is horizontal

slow reaction – gentle curve

fast reaction – steep curve

Making more product

Increasing the speed of a reaction will not make more product. It just means that the reaction finishes more quickly. The only way to make more product is to use more reactants.

Now do this

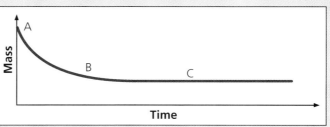

3 The graph shows the way the mass of marble chips changes during a reaction with acid.

a Which letter shows where the reaction is fastest? Explain why.

b Which letter shows where the reaction has stopped?

Fractionating oil

Many of the chemicals that we use in everyday life are made from oil. Crude oil is a mixture of liquids which boil at different temperatures. The liquids are separated by using **fractional distillation**.

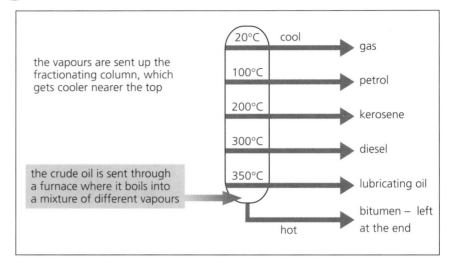

the vapours are sent up the fractionating column, which gets cooler nearer the top

the crude oil is sent through a furnace where it boils into a mixture of different vapours

As each vapour reaches the part of the column that is just below its own boiling point, that vapour will condense. The liquids with the highest boiling point condense low down the column where it is hottest and the liquids with the lowest boiling point rise up to the cooler part. The column has exit points at different levels so that the different boiling point liquids can drain out.

Now do this

1   What are the boiling points of diesel fuel, petrol and kerosene?

2   Why does petrol leave the fractionating column higher up than kerosene?

3   Why does diesel fuel have a higher boiling point than petrol?

What is crude oil made of?

Crude oil is mainly made of hydrocarbons. Hydrocarbons are molecules made of hydrogen and carbon only. They have different numbers of carbon atoms inside their molecules. The more carbon atoms there are, the higher the boiling point.

One group of hydrocarbons is called the **alkanes**. Here are the first five alkanes.

methane, CH_4 ethane, C_2H_6 propane, C_3H_8 butane, C_4H_{10} pentane, C_5H_{12}

What is oil used for?

Some hydrocarbons are used to make other substances such as plastics. Most are burned as a fuel for transport, for heating and for cooking.

Hydrocarbons make good fuels because they transfer a lot of energy. When the fuel burns the energy can be used to make your car move or to heat your food.

- Methane is Natural Gas – used for heating, cooking and in Bunsen burners.
- Propane and butane are used for heating and for camping gas stoves.
- Paraffin is used for heating and for lamps.
- Petrol and diesel are used as fuels.

When a hydrocarbon burns with plenty of oxygen
- the hydrogen atoms form water
- the carbon atoms form carbon dioxide.

The reaction for methane burning in a gas cooker is:

$$CH_4 \quad + \quad 2O_2 \quad \rightarrow \quad CO_2 \quad + \quad 2H_2O$$
methane + oxygen → carbon dioxide + water

If there is not enough oxygen in the room the carbon in the hydrocarbons will form carbon monoxide instead of carbon dioxide. Carbon monoxide is poisonous and will kill you. Gas cookers and some gas fires are only safe if the room is well ventilated.

$$CH_4 \quad + \quad 1.5O_2 \quad \rightarrow \quad CO \quad + \quad 2H_2O$$
methane + oxygen → carbon monoxide + water

Oxidation

When something reacts with oxygen to make an oxide we say that it has been **oxidised**. This is an **oxidation** reaction.

Now do this

4 Copy and complete these sentences: Choose from the following words:

carbon dioxide   carbon   hydrogen   alkanes   oxidation   water

Oil contains a group of compounds called _____. These all contain two elements _____ and _____. When hydrocarbons burn in air they make _____ _____ and _____. This reaction with oxygen is called _____.

5 Write a word equation to show what happens when methane burns in oxygen.

Energy in reactions

Most chemical reactions transfer energy. The energy can be transferred in different ways. Burning is a chemical reaction which produces heat and light. When marble chips react with acid you can hear the 'fizz' which is energy being transferred as sound. The chemicals inside a battery produce electricity.

Exothermic and endothermic reactions

Reactions which get hot are **exothermic**, they give out energy. A few reactions take energy in as they happen, this makes them feel cold and they are called **endothermic** reactions.

Measuring the energy

You can tell how much energy has been transferred in an exothermic reaction by using the reaction to heat up some water. The hotter the water gets, the more energy transfer.

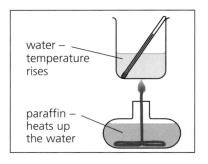

water – temperature rises

paraffin – heats up the water

The energy transferred from burning paraffin heats up water. Fossil fuel contains a lot of energy.

The reaction which gives the biggest temperature rise transfers the most energy. Remember to always use the same amount of water!

Energy is measured in joules, J or in kilojoules, kJ. There are 1000 joules in a kilojoule.

Now do this

Three fuels were burned to see which transferred the most energy.

Fuel	Starting temperature	Final temperature
A	20 °C	30 °C
B	20 °C	40 °C
C	25 °C	43 °C

1   Which fuel transferred the most energy?

2   Was the reaction exothermic or endothermic?

Energy and the environment

Burning fossil fuels produces two gases that cause a lot of pollution. The first is carbon dioxide, the other is sulphur dioxide. Carbon dioxide is a major cause of the greenhouse effect.

The greenhouse effect

Ultra-violet rays from the Sun go through the Earth's atmosphere and heat up the Earth's surface. The warm Earth gives off infra-red radiation. Greenhouse gases in the atmosphere trap some of the infra-red radiation and stop some of its energy getting out. This means that the Earth gets hotter.

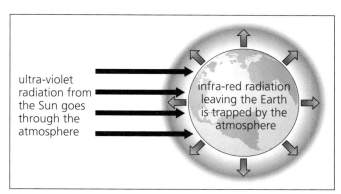

Carbon dioxide is the major greenhouse gas. Because we burn millions of tonnes of oil and coal every year carbon dioxide is being produced faster than it is being removed. This is slowly making the Earth warmer. Another greenhouse gas is methane, which is produced by farm animals and from rotting vegetation.

Sulphur dioxide and acid rain

Fossil fuels such as coal and oil contain carbon compounds and small amounts of sulphur. The sulphur turns into sulphur oxides when the fuel burns. These oxides dissolve in rain water to make acid rain. Acid rain can corrode buildings, and also changes the soil slightly which harms animals and plants.

There is more on hydrocarbon fuels on pages 23 and 102.

Now do this

3   What are the missing words? Choose from the following:

carbon dioxide   ultra-violet   infra-red   sulphur dioxide   greenhouse

When carbon compounds burn _____ gas is formed. This affects the temperature of the Earth so it is called a _____ gas. It lets _____ radiation from the Sun through the atmosphere but it won't let _____ radiation from the Earth back out again. Fossil fuels also contain small quantities of sulphur. This produces _____ _____ when it burns, which causes acid rain.

Air and carbon cycle

Air is a mixture of gases

Oxygen is one of the two most important gases in air, but it does not make up a large amount of the air. The air is made of approximately

- 80% nitrogen – which does very little
- 20% oxygen – a most important gas
- small amounts of other gases, including
- 0.04% carbon dioxide – the other important gas, even though there is only a very small amount of it.

The atmosphere also contains large amounts of water vapour, but the amount changes with the weather.

The amounts of nitrogen and oxygen never change much because they are being made at about the same rate as they are being used up. The amount of carbon dioxide is also fairly constant. Some people believe that levels of carbon dioxide are increasing very slowly because it is being made slightly faster than it is being used up.

What happens to the carbon dioxide?

- Carbon dioxide from the atmosphere is taken in by plants during photosynthesis.
- Carbon goes from the plants to the animals when the animals eat the plants.
- Carbon dioxide goes back into the atmosphere when plants and animals respire.
- Carbon dioxide goes back into the atmosphere when plants, such as trees, burn (combustion).
- If the animals or plants turn into fossil fuels, such as coal and oil, the fuel forms carbon dioxide when it burns.
- If the animals form rocks, such as chalk, their carbon is locked away in the rock.

Test for carbon dioxide

Carbon dioxide turns lime water milky.

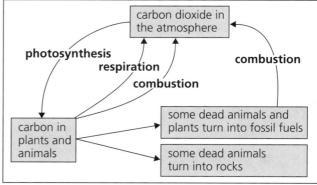

Now do this

1   What are the two main processes that put carbon dioxide into the atmosphere?
2   What is the main process that takes carbon dioxide out of the atmosphere?

Where did the air come from?

Billions of years ago there was no oxygen in the Earth's atmosphere. Life did not exist. The atmosphere was formed by volcanoes which were producing ammonia, methane, carbon dioxide and water.

Three billion years ago the first simple plant life appeared. The plants turned the carbon dioxide and water into food and oxygen – photosynthesis had started.

At first, all the oxygen produced by the plants reacted with iron in the rocks. Once all the iron had reacted with oxygen, oxygen started going into the atmosphere.

The amount of oxygen in the atmosphere increased. The different types of living things increased until the living things were using up the oxygen as fast as it was being made. This now keeps the amount of oxygen constant.

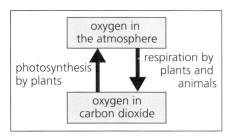

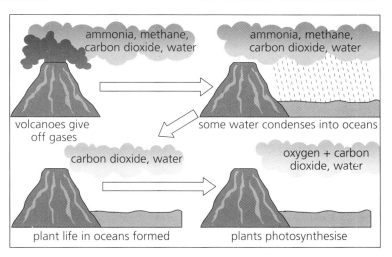

Where did the oceans come from?

When the Earth formed there was water vapour coming out of volcanoes. As the Earth cooled the water vapour condensed and turned into rain which formed the oceans. The rain dissolved chemicals such as salt out of the rocks, so sea water contains a mixture of different chemicals dissolved in it.

Now do this

3 Copy out this sentence, filling in the missing words. Choose from:

combustion   respiration   oxygen   20%   80%   carbon dioxide   0.04%

The atmosphere is made of _____ nitrogen, _____ oxygen and _____ carbon dioxide. Plants produce _____ gas during photosynthesis; it is needed for respiration and things burn in it. Respiration is very similar to burning because they both produce _____ gas. The amounts of carbon dioxide and oxygen in the atmosphere stay fairly constant because the rate of photosynthesis is balanced by _____ and _____.

The Earth's crust

What is the Earth made of?

The top layer of the Earth is a thin rocky **crust**.

The **mantle** is under the crust. It is made of very hot solid rock that can slowly move. It can melt into **magma**, a molten rock. In the middle of the Earth is the **core**. The Earth's core is even hotter than the Earth's mantle and is liquid.

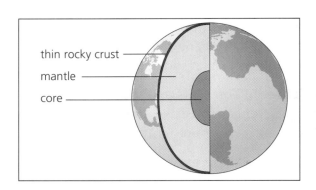

Plate tectonics

The shapes of the continents of Africa and South America fit together like a jigsaw. They also have similar rocks and fossils on the coasts that face each other. This is because they were once joined together.

The thin rocky crust of the Earth is made up of large, slowly moving sections called plates. The plates move a few centimetres each year and they may be moving away from each other or into each other.

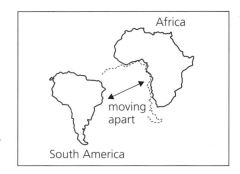

The forces created where the plates move against each other are so strong that the edges of the plates are marked by earthquakes, volcanoes and mountain ranges.

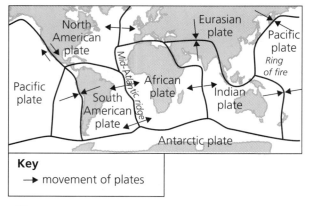

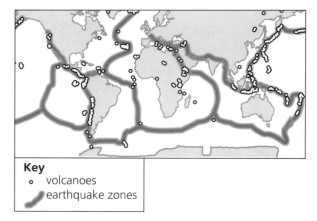

![??? Now do this]

Now do this

The Pacific Plate is surrounded by a ring of volcanoes called 'The ring of fire'.

1   Find the volcanoes on the map.

2   How far are the volcanoes from the edges of the plates?

3   How far are the earthquake zones from the edges of the plates?

The movement of plates

When plates move together one plate is forced underneath the other. As it is pushed down into the mantle the rock melts. Rocks on the surface get pushed up into mountain ranges.

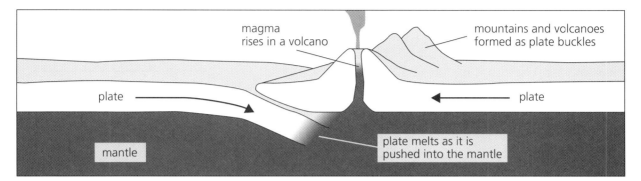

What happens when plates move apart?

The Atlantic Ocean is getting wider by at least a centimetre every year. This is because the plates on either side are moving apart, leaving a gap down the centre of the ocean floor. Magma flows into the gap, making a ridge of new rocks. This is called sea floor spreading. There are earthquakes and sometimes volcanoes, as a result of sea floor spreading.

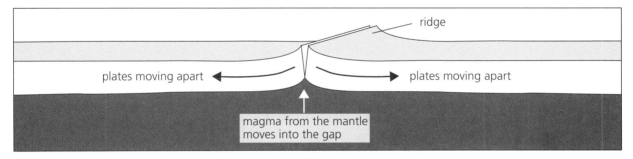

Scientists first realised that the sea floor was spreading when they found out that as you go further from the ridge the rocks get older.

Now do this

4 When two plates push into each other, one plate stays on the surface and the other plate disappears.
   a Where does this plate go?
   b What happens to the rocks of that plate?

5 What happens to the age of the rocks as you move away from a place where the sea floor is spreading?

Rock formation

How are rocks formed?

Igneous rocks are made from magma which has cooled down and solidified. It usually forms interlocking crystals of different **minerals**.

Sedimentary rocks are small pieces of older rock, for example sand or mud, which settle. The layers at the bottom are compressed by the weight of the layers above them, which helps turn them into a solid rock. Often, chemicals soaking through the rock will also cement the grains together.

Examples of sedimentary rock are shale, which is made from mud; conglomerate, which is made from pebbles; and sandstone, which is made from grains of sand. Sedimentary rocks can also be made from bits of animal or plant, for example limestone is made from sea shells, coal is made from prehistoric trees. Rock salt is made when seawater evaporates and leaves the salt behind.

Metamorphic rocks are rocks which have changed after they were originally formed. This is usually caused by high temperature or pressure from other rocks. Marble and slate are metamorphic rocks.

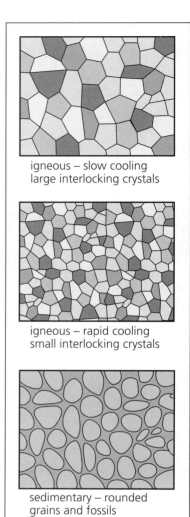

igneous – slow cooling
large interlocking crystals

igneous – rapid cooling
small interlocking crystals

sedimentary – rounded
grains and fossils

Oil and natural gas

As microscopic sea creatures die and settle on the sea bed some are covered in sediment which eventually turns to rock. The solid sediments keep out air, and the pressure and high temperature 90–120°C of the layer of rock forms oil from the dead creatures. The oil soaks up through the rocks until it reaches a layer of **non-permeable rock** that it can't soak through. If that layer of non-permeable rock is the right shape – an oil trap – the oil will stay in the rocks just under the layer.

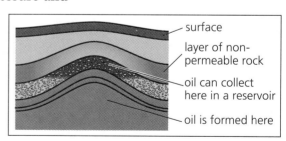

surface

layer of non-permeable rock

oil can collect here in a reservoir

oil is formed here

Now do this

1 What are the missing words? Choose from:

**igneous   large
metamorphic**

Granite rock is made from magma which cools slowly underground. This means that it will have _____ size crystals. It is a _____ type of rock. If rocks are then put under great pressure or temperature they will change to _____ rock.

The rock cycle

Rocks are continually being broken down into pieces. This is called **weathering**. Weathering happens if rocks get very hot then very cold as in a desert. This makes them expand and contract until they shatter. This is called **exfoliation**. Weathering also happens when water gets into cracks in the rock and freezes. The water expands when it freezes and splits the rock. This is called **freeze-thaw**.

The pieces are then carried away by the wind or by streams and rivers. This is called **transportation**. The pieces hit each other as they move and their jagged edges are rounded off.

Eventually the pieces settle, are buried and solidify into layers of **sedimentary rock**. Earth movements can then bring the rock back to the surface so that it is weathered all over again.

Earth movements can bring any of the three types of rock up to the surface, where they will be weathered and eventually form sedimentary rock.

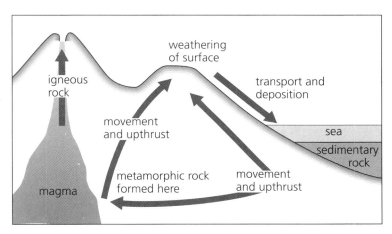

The age of sedimentary rocks

Usually the oldest rocks form the bottom layer in sedimentary rock and the youngest rocks form the top layer..

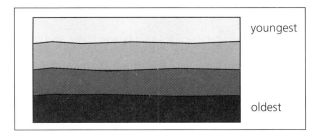

Now do this

2   Copy and complete these sentences. Choose from the following words:

upthrust   metamorphic   sedimentary   weathering

Rocks on the surface are slowly broken into small pieces. This is called _____.
The pieces are carried to the sea where they settle and turn into _____ rock.
If that rock is put under great pressure or temperature it will change into
_____ rock. It can appear back on the Earth's surface because of _____.

Metals from rocks

The metals we use come from rocks. A few are found as the metal itself, but most metals are combined with other elements such as oxygen or sulphur.

Iron, for example, is often found as iron oxide. Iron oxide mixed with rock is iron ore.

To get metals away from their ores we have to remove the oxygen. We can do this by using a more reactive element to take away the oxygen.

Reactivity

The most reactive elements form bonds with other elements which are hard to break. The least reactive elements form bonds which are easy to break, or do not form bonds at all.

We can list the elements in order of their reactivity. Sodium, calcium, magnesium and zinc are all very reactive. They will bond tightly with oxygen from the air, they react with water and with acids. Sodium and calcium are so reactive that it is too dangerous to put them with acids!

Less reactive metals such as copper and silver don't react with water or acids. Copper is used to make water pipes because it doesn't corrode in water and silver is used for jewellery. Copper and silver will only react with oxygen if they are heated, and even so they don't stick very tightly to the oxygen.

Reactivity series
most reactive
sodium
calcium
magnesium
aluminium
carbon
zinc
iron
hydrogen
copper
silver
least reactive

Metals reacting with other compounds

Reactive metals can steal substances away from less reactive metals.

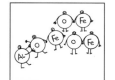

Aluminium is more reactive than iron, so it can steal the oxygen from the iron oxide:

aluminium + iron oxide → aluminium oxide + iron

Zinc is more reactive than copper, so it can steal the sulphate from copper sulphate:

zinc + copper sulphate → zinc sulphate + copper

Carbon is more reactive than iron and zinc, so that means that carbon will take oxygen away from iron oxide and from zinc oxide.

Now do this

1   Complete the equation

    zinc + copper oxide → _____ + _____

2 a Which of these will hydrogen react with: iron oxide, copper oxide, silver oxide?

  b What will be formed in the cases that do react?

Extracting elements from their minerals – reduction

Carbon is a very useful substance for taking oxygen away from metals. It is fairly cheap and it is more reactive than iron and copper, which we have to extract in very large quantities. This means that carbon can take iron out of iron ore.

Any reaction that takes oxygen away from an oxide is called a **reduction reaction**.

Iron is extracted from iron ore using carbon in a blast furnace. Carbon is converted into carbon monoxide and it is the carbon monoxide which actually does the reduction.

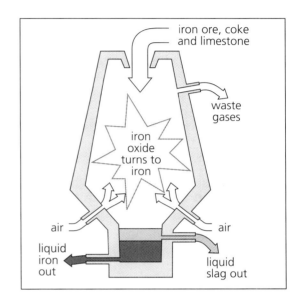

Iron ore and coke are put in at the top of the furnace and air is pumped through the holes at the side. There is so much heat given out in this reaction that the iron melts and collects at the bottom of the furnace. Limestone is used to react with impurities in the iron ore and turn them into liquid slag. The slag floats on top of the iron and is drained out of the furnace before the liquid iron is run out.

Carbon and oxygen form carbon monoxide.

carbon	+	oxygen	$\rightarrow$ carbon monoxide
2C	+	O_2	$\rightarrow$ 2CO

Carbon monoxide takes the oxygen from the iron oxide.

carbon monoxide	+ iron oxide	$\rightarrow$	carbon dioxide	+ iron
3CO	+ Fe_2O_3	$\rightarrow$	$3CO_2$	+ 2Fe

 Now do this

3 What do we call the reaction that takes oxygen away from something?

4 Carbon will take oxygen from copper oxide. Write a word equation for this.

5 a Which would you expect to corrode in air most quickly, iron or zinc?

b Explain why.

Ions, ionic bonds and electrolysis

Atoms are neutral. An atom can become charged, but as
soon as this happens it is called an **ion**. Atoms turn into
ions by **gaining electrons** or by **losing electrons**.

If an atom gains electrons it becomes a **negative** ion.
If an atom gives away electrons it becomes a **positive** ion.

A chlorine atom gains one electron, forming a chloride ion	Cl	→	Cl^-
An oxygen atom gains two electrons, forming an oxide ion	O	→	O^{2-}
A sodium atom gives away one electron, forming a sodium ion	Na	→	Na^+
A calcium atoms gives away two electrons, forming a calcium ion	Ca	→	Ca^{2+}

Ionic compounds

If an atom gives one or more electrons to another atom
they both form ions. The ions have opposite charges, so
they will attract each other; this is called **ionic bonding**.
When sodium reacts with chlorine each sodium atom
gives an electron to a chlorine atom. Each sodium atom
forms a positive ion, Na^+, each chlorine atom forms a
negative ion, Cl^-. Na^+ and Cl^- will now form ionic bonds
because of their opposite charges.

Electrolysis

Ionic compounds will conduct electricity if they are
melted or dissolved. This is because the ions can move in
a liquid, so the ions can carry the charge through the
liquid. Ionic solids don't conduct because the particles in
a solid are held in one place.

Ions are attracted by the oppositely
charged electrode. The cathode is
negative and attracts positive ions.
The anode is positive and attracts
negative ions.

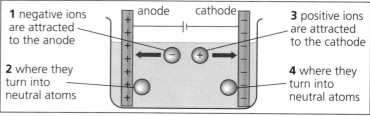

1 negative ions are attracted to the anode
2 where they turn into neutral atoms
anode   cathode
3 positive ions are attracted to the cathode
4 where they turn into neutral atoms

Now do this

1   Metals give away electrons. What sort of charges do their ions have?

2   Some non-metals can gain electrons. What sort of charges do their ions have?

3   Magnesium atoms lose two electrons. Write the symbol for a magnesium ion.

4   Solid sodium chloride is ionic. Why doesn't it conduct electricity?

5   Which electrode will metal ions go towards during electrolysis?

Using electrolysis to extract aluminium

Aluminium ore contains aluminium oxide. Aluminium is very reactive. It bonds tightly to oxygen, so we can't use carbon to take the oxygen away from the oxide. Instead we use cryolite as a solvent to dissolve the aluminium oxide in. The cryolite lowers the melting point of aluminium oxide and so saves energy.

The sides and the bottom of the tank are lined with carbon. This is connected to an electricity supply to make the cathode. The anodes are also made of carbon. They are lowered into the molten mixture of aluminium oxide and cryolite.

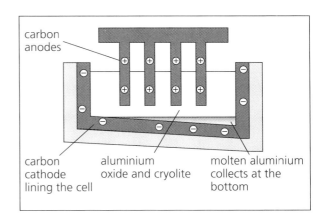

Aluminium ions are positive, so they are attracted to the negative cathode and gains electrons. Molten aluminium collects at the bottom of the tank. Oxygen is given off at the carbon anodes.

Using electrolysis to purify or extract copper

- The anode is the impure copper.
- The cathode is a pure copper plate.
- During electrolysis the copper dissolves from the impure anode and plates on to the cathode.
- The pure copper cathode becomes thicker as more copper plates on to it.

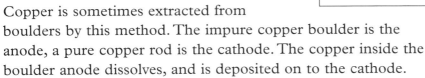

Copper is sometimes extracted from boulders by this method. The impure copper boulder is the anode, a pure copper rod is the cathode. The copper inside the boulder anode dissolves, and is deposited on to the cathode.

??? Now do this

6 What is the charge on
 a an anode   b a cathode?
7 Which electrode does aluminium collect at when aluminium oxide is electrolysed?
8 Which electrode does copper collect at when it is purified by electrolysis?

Metal objects can be electroplated by being made into the cathode in a copper sulphate solution. Copper ions are attracted to the cathode and turn into copper atoms on the side of the object.

Molecules and giants

Atoms can join together in small groups called molecules or in enormous groups called giant structures.

Molecules

Molecules are made of a few atoms bonded together. The atoms might all be the same, a molecule of an element, or they might be different, a molecule of a compound. The atoms are held together by strong chemical bonds.

Here are some of them. The lines between the atoms show where the bonds are.

hydrogen H_2	chlorine Cl_2	hydrogen chloride HCl	hydrogen oxide H_2O	methane CH_4
H—H	Cl—Cl	H—Cl	$H/^O\backslash H$	H—C—H (H above, H below)

Giant structures

Sometimes billions of atoms bond together into one group. This is a giant structure. The atoms inside the giant structure might all be the same, which is an element with a giant structure. The particles might be different, which is a compound with a giant structure.

Carbon is famous because it is an element that has two different forms; diamond and graphite. Diamond and graphite are both giant structures.

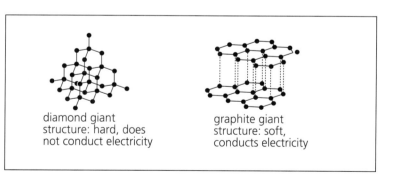

diamond giant structure: hard, does not conduct electricity

graphite giant structure: soft, conducts electricity

Now do this

1 How many atoms are in one methane molecule?

2 How many elements are in a methane molecule?

How can you tell if it is a molecular structure?

It will have a low boiling point.
A 'low' boiling point is anything under 500°C.

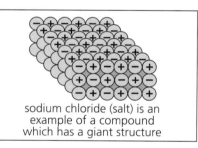

sodium chloride (salt) is an example of a compound which has a giant structure

How can you tell if it is a giant structure?

It will have a high melting point.

The particles are all bonded to each other, this makes it hard to melt the solid.

 Now do this

3 A solid melts at 100°C. What type of structure has it got?

4 A solid melts at 1000°C. What sort of structure has it got?

Other carbon compounds

There are millions of carbon compounds. Some of them are very similar, so we put them into groups. The two groups that you need to know are the alkanes and the alkenes. Both groups are made of carbon and hydrogen only, so they are both hydrocarbons.

Alkanes

The first alkanes in the group are shown below.

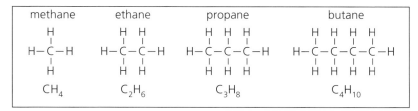

Now do this

5   How many carbon atoms are in a propane molecule?

As the alkane molecule gets bigger the boiling point increases. The alkanes all burn well with a clean blue flame.

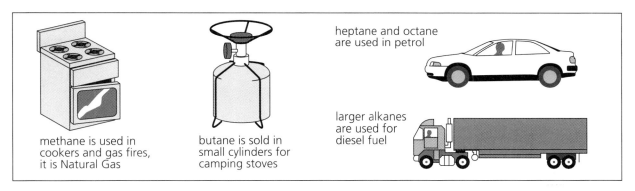

heptane and octane are used in petrol

larger alkanes are used for diesel fuel

methane is used in cookers and gas fires, it is Natural Gas

butane is sold in small cylinders for camping stoves

We get the alkanes from crude oil. Crude oil never has the 'right' amounts of the different alkanes that we need. There aren't enough small alkanes to make petrol, so we 'crack' the larger alkane molecules using a catalyst, high temperatures and high pressure. Cracking also produces hydrogen which is used in the Haber process.

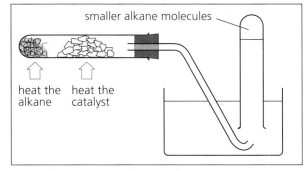

smaller alkane molecules

heat the alkane   heat the catalyst

Now do this

6 a Write a word equation for methane burning in oxygen.

   b Now turn it into a balanced chemical equation.

Making useful products

All manufactured materials and goods come from raw materials.
Many of these raw materials come from the Earth's crust and atmosphere.

ethene

$$\begin{array}{cc} H & H \\ | & | \\ C & = C \\ | & | \\ H & H \end{array}$$

Using alkenes

When crude oil is distilled, alkenes are produced as well as
alkanes. The simplest alkene is ethene, C_2H_4. It is sometimes
written as shown on the right. This is not the same as ethane.

Plastics

Alkenes are often used to make plastics. Plastics are made of
small molecules which are joined together into long chains. The
small molecules are called **monomers**, the large molecule is a
polymer. Polymerisation often needs high pressures and a catalyst.
The alkenes are good monomers. Different alkenes make different
types of plastic which are used to do different jobs.

monomer	+	monomer	+	monomer	→	polymer
M	+	**M**	+	**M**	→	–M–M–M–

Ethene is the monomer used to make poly(ethene), or polythene.

ethene + ethene + ethene + ethene → poly(ethene)

Polythene is cheap and flexible, so it is used to make polythene bags.

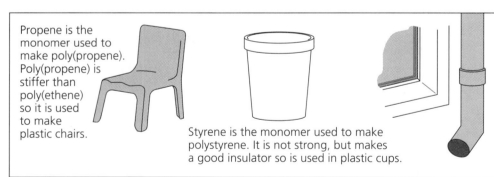

Propene is the monomer used to make poly(propene). Poly(propene) is stiffer than poly(ethene) so it is used to make plastic chairs.

Styrene is the monomer used to make polystyrene. It is not strong, but makes a good insulator so is used in plastic cups.

Vinyl chloride is the monomer used to make poly(vinyl chloride) – PVC. PVC is not as cheap as polythene but it lasts better outdoors, so it is used for drainpipes and window frames, as well as records.

Other plastics are used for packaging,
insulation, plastic drainpipes and so on. One
problem with plastics is that when they are
thrown away they are not attacked by
decomposers in the soil, so they do not rot
like most rubbish. Plastics are **non-biodegradable**. Some modern plastics have
now been produced which will rot when they
are thrown away, so these are **biodegradable**.

 Now do this

1 Write the formula of **a** ethane;
b ethene.

2 Write a word equation like the
one for poly(ethene) to show
how polystyrene is made.

Enzymes and biotechnology

Catalysts are important in a wide range of industrial processes. In some important industries the catalysts used are **enzymes**. Enzymes are biological catalysts which are produced inside living things.

Like other catalysts, specific enzymes are needed for specific reactions. Unlike other catalysts, enzymes are quickly damaged by temperatures that are too high for them. All reactions go faster as they get hotter, but if an enzyme is involved the reaction will only get faster up to a certain temperature, then it will slow down or stop as the enzyme is damaged.

Using enzymes

Enzymes are important in the baking, brewing and dairy industries. Yeast is used in both baking and brewing because the yeast cells contain enzymes which convert sugar into carbon dioxide and alcohol during fermentation.

sugar → alcohol + carbon dioxide

Brewers use yeast for the alcohol, bakers use it for the carbon dioxide. In each case the yeast needs sugar, moisture and warm conditions to work.

Controlling enzymes in the kitchen

Some enzymes are a problem because they make fresh food decay. Apples go brown when you cut them open because an enzyme speeds up the reaction of the apple with the air. Enzymes can be controlled by:

- cooking – this destroys the enzyme and stops the food decaying so fast
- refrigeration – this does not destroy the enzymes, but the low temperature slows down any reactions so it keeps food fresh for a short time
- freezing – this does not destroy the enzymes, but it stops any reactions so it is a good way of keeping food fresh for a long time.

Baking

Sugar and yeast are added to bread dough so that the enzymes in the yeast can produce bubbles of carbon dioxide. When it is cooked the dough solidifies round the bubbles, giving bread an open texture. The high temperature of the cooking kills the yeast and drives off the carbon dioxide and the alcohol.

Brewing

Yeast is added to grape juice to make wine, and to barley grains to make beer. The enzymes in the yeast convert the sugars into alcohol during fermentation. The carbon dioxide bubbles out of the liquid.

Dairy industry

The enzyme rennin makes milk clot and form cheese, and enzymes in bacteria are used to convert milk to yoghurt.

Now do this

3 What happens to the speed of a reaction involving an enzyme:
   a if you start to heat it up?
   b if you heat it further?

4 When yeast ferments it converts sugar into two chemicals. What are they?

5 Give **two different** uses for sugar.

Acids and pH

Natural acids are all around us. Acids in orange juice and vinegar give a sharp sour taste. Acids in nettles and bee stings hurt us. Acids in our stomachs help digest our food.

How acidic is it?

An indicator such as damp litmus paper will tell you if something is acidic – it will turn from blue to red. The pH scale tells us more, it tells us how strongly acidic something is.

The pH scale

very acidic						slightly acidic	NEUTRAL	slightly alkaline				very alkaline		
0	1	2	3	4	5	6	7	8	9	10	11	12	13	14

Acids from the lab such as hydrochloric acid or sulphuric acid have a pH of about 1, so they are very acidic. Lemon juice and vinegar are much less acidic with a pH of around 4. Sodium hydroxide is at the other end, and has a pH of about 14, but baking soda is usually around pH 8.

Bases, alkalis and neutralisation

A **base** is a metal oxide which reacts with an acid to form a salt and water.

A base which will dissolve in water is an **alkali**. Sodium hydroxide is an alkali. When an acid and a base react completely they **neutralise** each other, there is no acid or base left at the end.

When alkalis react with acids they produce a **salt** and water. Acids always form salts when they react. Some fertilisers are salts that are made by neutralising acid with ammonia.

acid + alkali → salt + water

Metal oxides and hydroxides are usually bases, non-metal oxides are usually acidic.

Acids and metals

Many metals react with acids, they are bases. The acid gives off its hydrogen and the rest of the acid turns into a salt.

acid + metal → salt + hydrogen

Not all metals react with acids.

If you put acid into a beaker of alkali the pH in the beaker will start high and drop to pH 7 when the acid and alkali have neutralised each other. If you put too much acid into the beaker the pH will pass the neutral point and go below 7!

Now do this

1. What pH numbers are alkaline?

2. What pH number is neutral?

3. Which is more acidic, pH 3 or 6?

4. Bee stings are acidic. Choose the best substance from the list under the pH scale to neutralise the sting.

Acid + metal carbonates

Carbonates react with acids to make a salt, water and carbon dioxide gas. The carbon dioxide forms bubbles, the salt usually dissolves so you can't see it.

acid + carbonate → salt + water + carbon dioxide

Marble chips are made of calcium carbonate.

hydrochloric + calcium → calcium + water + carbon
acid　　　　　carbonate　chloride　　　　　　　dioxide

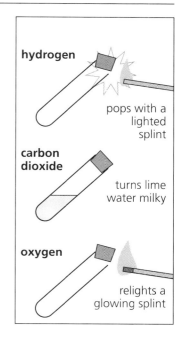

hydrogen — pops with a lighted splint

carbon dioxide — turns lime water milky

oxygen — relights a glowing splint

Acids and fertilisers

One of the most valuable uses of neutralisation is in making ammonia based fertilisers. These fertilisers give plants more nitrogen so that they grow faster and bigger. The nitrogen needs to be in a soluble form for the plants to take it up through their roots.

Ammonia [NH_3] is a suitable form but when it dissolves in water it forms an alkali which damages plants. So it is neutralised with acid to make an ammonium salt. Sulphuric acid will make ammonium sulphate, nitric acid (which is made from ammonia by another process) makes ammonium nitrate.

Ammonium sulphate and ammonium nitrate are common fertilisers.

acid + alkali → salt + water
sulphuric acid + ammonium hydroxide → ammonium sulphate + water
nitric acid + ammonium hydroxide → ammonium nitrate + water

Pollution and fertilisers

Rain water runs off farmers' fields into lakes and ponds, carrying fertilisers with it. The lakes and ponds are polluted as the fertiliser increases the growth of microscopic plants which cut off the light to the rest of the pond, making everything else in the pond die. This is called **eutrophication**.

In some areas of the country the amount of fertiliser draining into the rivers is causing too high a level of nitrates in the drinking water, which could be dangerous to babies.

Now do this

Marble chips are made of calcium carbonate.

5　What gas is formed when you add acid?

6　What would you see when you added the acid?

7　How would you test the gas?

8　Which fertiliser is made if you use ammonium hydroxide and sulphuric acid?

9　What causes eutrophication?

Reversible reactions

Some reactions will go in both directions. If you put acid with pH indicator, the indicator will turn red. If you now add alkali the indicator changes to blue. Add acid again, and it goes back to red.

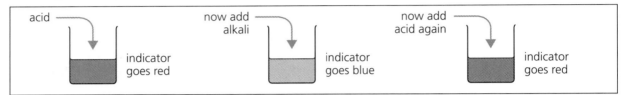

acid → indicator goes red

now add alkali → indicator goes blue

now add acid again → indicator goes red

You can do this as many times as you want. The reaction will go in either direction just as easily.

Usually it is very difficult to make a reaction go backwards but in this case it is very easy. We call this type of reaction a **reversible reaction**.

Making ammonia

Ammonia is made from nitrogen and hydrogen in a reversible reaction.

$$\text{nitrogen} + \text{hydrogen} \rightleftharpoons \text{ammonia}$$
$$N_2 + 3H_2 \rightleftharpoons 2NH_3$$

When you mix nitrogen and hydrogen a small amount of ammonia is produced. But it immediately starts to turn back to nitrogen and hydrogen. The reaction goes in both directions at the same time.

Eventually the forward reaction is going at the same speed as the backward reaction. From this point onwards there will not be any change in the amount of chemicals, they have reached a balance point. This is an **equilibrium**.

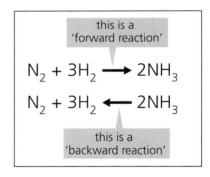

this is a 'forward reaction'

$$N_2 + 3H_2 \longrightarrow 2NH_3$$
$$N_2 + 3H_2 \longleftarrow 2NH_3$$

this is a 'backward reaction'

The Haber process

Millions of tons of ammonia are produced every year so that we can make fertiliser. The method of making ammonia is called the Haber process after the man who discovered it.

Hydrogen is made by cracking hydrocarbons from crude oil, and nitrogen is taken from the air. To make the hydrogen and the nitrogen react we use a high pressure, a high temperature, and a catalyst to speed it up. The catalyst is iron, a transition metal.

Now do this

1 What is a reversible reaction?

2 What is produced if you put an iron catalyst with ammonia?

How much do we need?

If you want to carry out a chemical reaction without wasting any of the chemicals you need to know just how much of each reactant you need to start off with. We can work this out from the equation for the reaction.

For example, the equation for iron reacting with sulphur is

$$Fe + S \rightarrow FeS$$

One atom of iron reacts with one atom of sulphur to make iron sulphide.

But atoms of different elements weigh different amounts. You can see how much the different atoms weigh by looking at their relative atomic masses given in the **periodic table**.

Hydrogen is the lightest element, so it has a relative atomic mass = 1. Sulphur atoms are heavier, they have a relative atomic mass of 32. Iron atoms are heavier still at 56. This means that 32 grams of sulphur react exactly with 56 grams of iron.

Another reaction could be the reaction of hydrogen with chlorine. For one atom of hydrogen to react with one atom of chlorine, you will need 1 gram of hydrogen for every 35.5 grams of chlorine.

Relative atomic masses

hydrogen	H	= 1
carbon	C	= 12
nitrogen	N	= 14
oxygen	O	= 16
sodium	Na	= 23
sulphur	S	= 32
chlorine	Cl	= 35.5
iron	Fe	= 56

 Now do this

3 You have 1 g of hydrogen. You want the same number of atoms of carbon. How much do you weigh out? You want twice as many atoms of oxygen. How much do you weigh out?

4 You have 2 g of hydrogen. You want the same number of atoms of chlorine. How much do you weigh out? You want twice as many atoms of carbon. How much do you weigh out?

Formula masses

When we weigh out substances made of more than one atom, we have to add up the masses of all the atoms inside the formula. This is called the formula mass.

 Now do this

5a What is the formula mass of NH_3?
b What is the formula mass of H_2O?
c What is the formula mass of NaOH?

A hydrogen molecule is H_2	The formula mass for H_2 is	1 + 1	= 2
An oxygen molecule is O_2	The formula mass for O_2 is	16 + 16	= 32
A methane molecule is CH_4	The formula mass for CH_4 is	12 + 1 + 1 + 1 + 1	= 32
Sodium chloride is NaCl	The formula mass for NaCl is	23 + 35.5	= 58.5

Atoms and isotopes

An atom is made of a tiny positive nucleus surrounded by shells of electrons.

The nucleus is made of protons and neutrons. Protons have a positive charge. Neutrons are neutral. They are both heavy particles.

The electrons fit in shells around the nucleus. They have a negative charge and weigh almost nothing.

Atoms are neutral. Their negative and positive charges cancel out. This means that the number of electrons must be the same as the number of protons.

Name	Charge	Mass	Where found
proton	+1	1	inside the nucleus
neutron	0	1	inside the nucleus
electron	−1	0	outside the nucleus, in shells

The number of protons in an atom is called the **atomic number** or the **proton number**. It tells you what element you have got. If an atom has one proton, the element is hydrogen, two protons means helium and so on.

The mass of an atom is made up of all the protons and neutrons, because they are both heavy. Add the two numbers together to make the **mass number**. The electrons don't weigh enough to matter.

We write all this information in a standard way.

The number of neutrons is the mass number minus the proton number.

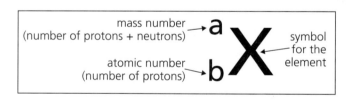

mass number (number of protons + neutrons) → a

atomic number (number of protons) → b

X

symbol for the element

Isotopes

Different forms of the same element are called **isotopes**. The only difference between them is the number of neutrons in the nucleus. One isotope is heavier than the other, but it has little other effect.

$^{12}_{6}C$ has 6 protons, so it is carbon. Work out how many neutrons it must have (mass number – proton number). You should have got the answer to be 6 neutrons.

$^{14}_{6}C$ has 6 protons, so it is carbon. Work out how many neutrons it must have (mass number – proton number). You should have got the answer to be 8 neutrons.

Now do this

1 What is the difference between $^{16}_{8}O$ and $^{18}_{8}O$?

2 How many protons are in $^{56}_{26}Fe$. How many neutrons are in $^{56}_{26}Fe$?

How are the electrons arranged in an atom?

In a neutral atom the number of electrons outside the nucleus is the same as the number of protons inside the nucleus. Electrons are negative, protons are positive, so the two sets of charges cancel out and the atom is neutral.

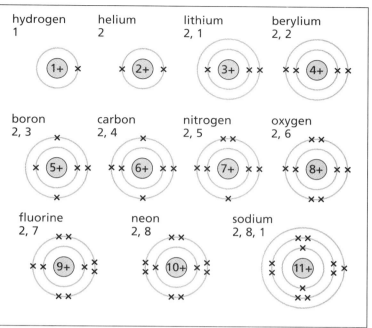

Electrons fit into shells around the nucleus. Two electrons fit into the first shell, then up to eight electrons fit into the next shell. Eight electrons is a stable number for all shells after the innermost shell.

Sodium has 11 electrons, so its electron arrangement is 2, 8, 1. This means that there are 2 electrons in the first shell, 8 in the next and 1 in the outer shell.

The number of electrons in the outer shell decides what sort of chemical reactions an element will have. Only the number in the outer shell is important.

Ions

Elements which are only one or two electrons away from the eight will form ions, they give electrons away or take them in so that they end up with the eight. If more than two electrons are involved the elements don't usually form ions when they react, they share electrons instead.

Elements whose atoms gain electrons to form ions

If 7 electrons in the outer shell gain one electron → 1^- ion.

If 6 electrons in the outer shell gain two electrons → 2^- ion.

Elements whose atoms give away electrons to form ions

If 1 electron in the outer shell gives away one electron → 1^+ ion,

If 2 electrons in the outer shell give away two electrons → 2^+ ion.

Now do this

3 Nitrogen has 7 protons in its nucleus.
 a How many electrons has it got?
 b How are the electrons arranged?

4 Sodium has 11 protons in its nucleus. What is its electron arrangement?

5 Potassium has 19 protons in its nucleus. What is its electron arrangement?

Periodic table

A periodic table will be printed on the back of your examination paper. It is a list of all the elements in order of their increasing proton numbers (atomic numbers). The order goes from left to right along each row, starting with the top row.

Elements which are similar fit into vertical lines called **groups**. The group numbers are written at the top of the table, they go from group I to group 0. Sometimes the last group on the right is called group VIII. Hydrogen is the one element that is sometimes not put into a group.

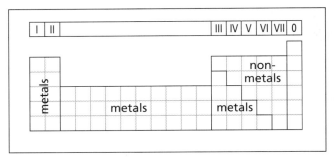

Metals and non-metals

There are two sorts of elements, metals and non-metals. The zig-zag line shows the boundary between them. Metals are on the left hand side of the table, non-metals are on the right.

The most reactive metals are at the bottom left. Non-metals often form acidic oxides. The most reactive non-metal, fluorine, is at the top of group VII.

Groups

The elements in a group are very similar because they all have the same number of electrons in their outer shell. The number of electrons in the outer shell is the same as the group number. Elements with one or two electrons in the outer shell will lose those electrons and form ions. Elements with six or seven electrons will gain electrons and form ions. There is a regular change in properties as you move down each group.

Group number	I	II	III	IV	V	VI	VII	0
Outer electrons	1	2	3	4	5	6	7	8
Ion formed	M^+	M^{2+}				X^{2-}	X^-	

Now do this

1 Find the proton number (atomic number) of sodium.

Metals will:
- react with oxygen to form oxides which are basic

Most metals will also:
- react with water to form hydrogen and oxides or hydroxides
- react with acids to form hydrogen and a salt.

Now do this

2 Explain why elements in group II form double positive ions.

3 Why don't group 0 elements form ions?

Group I: the alkali metals

The group I elements are called the **alkali metals**.
All you need to know about are the first three: lithium,
sodium and potassium.

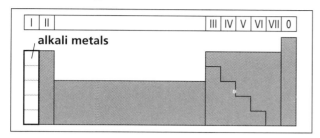

Element	Symbol	Relative atomic mass	Melting point
lithium	Li	7	180
sodium	Na	23	98
potassium	K	39	63

The group I metals:
- are soft, but shiny and conduct electricity
- form ions with a 1^+ charge as they lose the one electron in their outer shell
- get *more* reactive going down the group
- have lower melting and boiling points going down the group
- have low densities and so float on water
- react with oxygen in air and tarnish, so they are stored under oil to stop them reacting.

Reactions with water

All alkali metals float on water and react strongly to make alkaline solutions. (Use safety screen and goggles.) They force hydrogen gas out of the water and make the metal hydroxide.

> lithium + water → lithium hydroxide + hydrogen
> $2Li$ + $2H_2O$ → $2LiOH$ + H_2

The reaction gets more violent as you go down the group:
- lithium reacts but does not melt
- sodium melts and moves about the surface as it reacts
- potassium melts, moves about the surface and bursts into flame.

Alkali metal compounds have many uses:
- sodium chloride is table salt
- sodium hydrogen carbonate neutralises acid in upset stomachs
- potassium nitrate is a fertiliser.

Tests for alkali metals

The metals burn with coloured flames.

Lithium: red flame
Sodium: yellow flame
Potassium: lilac flame

Alkali metal compounds

Alkali metal compounds melt without breaking down at high temperatures. They dissolve in water and have colourless solutions.

Sodium carbonate is used in soap powder and to make sodium hydroxide. Sodium chloride is used to make chlorine and sodium hydroxide. Sodium hydroxide is used in making soap.

Now do this

4 Write a word equation for the reaction of sodium with water.

5 Write a balanced chemical equation for the reaction of sodium with water.

Group VII: the halogens

The group VII elements are called the **halogens**. All you need to know about are chlorine, bromine and iodine.

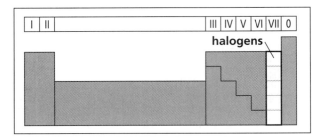

Element	Symbol	Relative atomic mass	Normal state	Colour
fluorine	F	19	gas	
chlorine	Cl	35.5	gas	green
bromine	Br	80	liquid	orange
iodine	I	127	solid	black

The group VII halogens:
- are poisonous acidic gases
- form ions with a 1$^-$ charge as they gain one electron to add to the 7 in their outer shell
- get *less* reactive going down the group
- have higher melting and boiling points going down the group
- react well with metals

  sodium + chlorine → sodium chloride

- their compounds usually dissolve in water
- halogens react with hydrogen to give acidic solutions

  hydrogen + chlorine → hydrogen chloride
  Hydrogen chloride, hydrogen bromide and hydrogen iodide are colourless gases which dissolve in water to give strongly acidic solutions. The solution of hydrogen chloride is hydrochloric acid.

Tests for halogens

To find out which halogen is in a compound, dissolve the compounds in water and add silver nitrate:

- chlorine compounds give a yellow precipitate
- bromine compounds give a cream precipitate
- iodine compounds give a yellow precipitate.

What are the halogens used for?

Chlorine is used: • as a bleach to get rid of stains • to kill bacteria in drinking water, swimming pools • to make plastics and insecticides • to make hydrochloric acid. This has many uses including etching metals and making plastics.	**Iodine** is an antiseptic. **Bromine** and **iodine** are used to make silver bromide and silver iodide. These chemicals turn black in sunlight, so they are used in photographic films.

Now do this

1 Write a word equation for the reaction between hydrogen and chlorine.

2 Sodium chloride has the formula NaCl. Write a balanced equation for the reaction between sodium and chlorine.

Group 0: the noble gases

The group 0 gases are called the **noble gases**. You need to
know about helium, neon, argon and krypton.

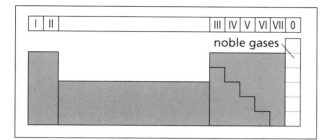

Element	Symbol	Relative atomic mass	Normal state
helium	He	4	gas
neon	Ne	20	gas
argon	Ar	40	gas
krypton	Kr	84	gas

The noble gases are helium, neon, argon, krypton, xenon and
radon. They are all colourless gases and have almost no
reactions at all. This is because they have a stable outer shell
(usually 8 electrons, except helium which has 2 electrons), so
they don't form any bonds. Although they are unreactive they
do show trends in their properties down the group. As their
atomic numbers increase down the group their boiling points
and densities increase.

Uses of the noble gases

Helium is used to fill balloons because it is less dense than air
and it will not burn. Neon, argon and krypton are used in
different sorts of lights, especially coloured 'neon' lights, and
in lasers. They are also used when an inert atmosphere is
needed – as a replacement for air if you have a chemical
which would react with air.

Now do this

1 Why are the noble gases so stable?

2 Which is denser, helium or krypton?

3 Give one use for argon.

Transition metals

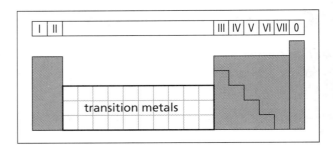

The **transition metals** contain the common metals such as iron and copper, silver and gold. They are all what we normally think of as metals – they conduct electricity and heat, they are shiny, hard, strong, dense and have high melting points. Most metals react with acids. Copper and iron are well known transition metals. Copper is used for water pipes and electric cables. Iron is used to make steel. Transition metals and their compounds can make good catalysts, for example iron is the catalyst in the Haber process for making ammonia.

Compounds of the transition metals

Most of the transition metal compounds are coloured. The colour is due to the metal ion inside the compound, so the colour tells you which transition element is present. The most famous is copper which forms blue and green compounds.

 Now do this

1 A metal
   A forms coloured compounds
   B conducts electricity
   C acts as a catalyst
   D reacts with acids

a Which **two** things show you that it is a metal?

b Which **two** things show you that the metal is probably a transition metal?

Concept map

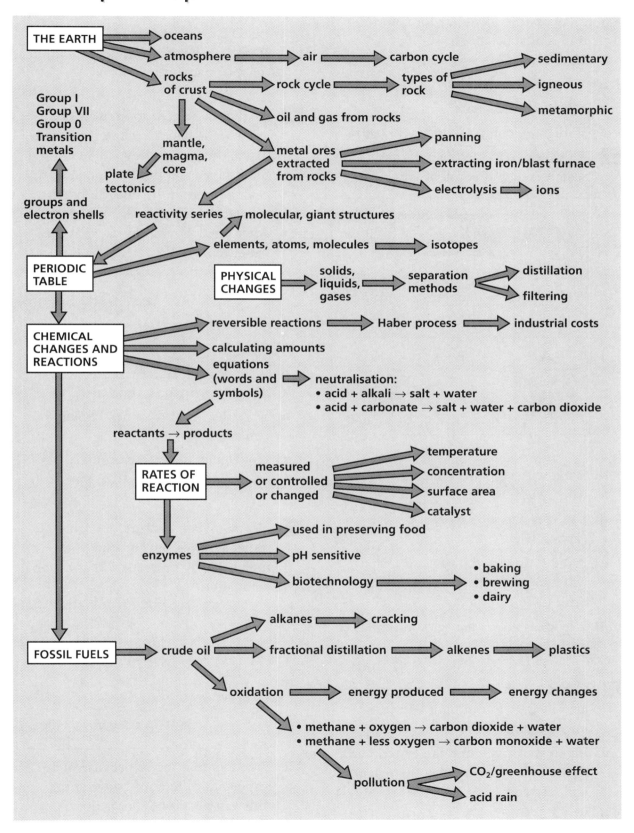

Exam questions

1 Here are the formulae for some different substances:

He   H$_2$ CH$_4$ S$_8$ H$_2$O

a Which are molecules?

b Which are elements?

c Which are compounds?   **[3 marks]**

2 The syringe in the diagram has a sealed end, and is full of air.

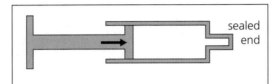

sealed end

a Which of these diagrams could show the particles in air?

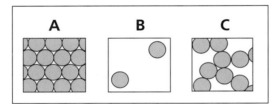

A   B   C

[1]

bi What will happen to the plunger when you push it?   [1]

ii Use ideas about particles in gases to explain why.   [2]

ci If the syringe is full of water, what will happen to the plunger when you push it?   [1]

ii Use ideas about particles in liquids to explain why.   [2]

[7 marks]

3 Calcium will react with oxygen if you heat it. It gives out light and turns into calcium oxide.

a If you were watching the experiment, how could you tell when the reaction had started?   [1]

b Write a word equation for this reaction.   [2]

c The symbols are calcium Ca, oxygen gas O$_2$, calcium oxide CaO. Write a balanced chemical equation for this reaction.   [2]

[5 marks]

4 A student wanted to know if two green pens had the same type of ink inside them. She drew a line on to a filter paper and put ink spots from each pen on to the line. She then dipped the filter paper into water. After a few hours, this is what the paper looked like.

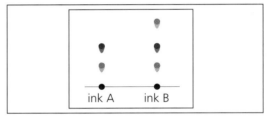

ink A   ink B

a What happened to the water?   [1]

b Were the inks the same? Explain how you can tell.   [1]

ci How many dyes were in ink A?   [1]

ii How many dyes were in ink B?   [1]

[4 marks]

5 Crude oil is a mixture of alkane molecules. We can separate these molecules by fractionation (fractional distillation).

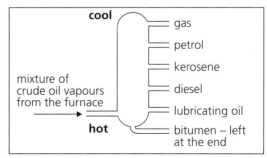

cool

gas

petrol

kerosene

mixture of crude oil vapours from the furnace

diesel

lubricating oil

hot

bitumen – left at the end

a Fractionation works because of an important difference between the different alkanes. What is this difference?   [1]

b Alkanes are made of carbon and hydrogen. When the alkanes such as petrol burn they react with oxygen in the atmosphere.

 i What do we call reactions where chemicals combine with oxygen?   [1]

 ii Name two chemicals that are made when petrol is burned in a plentiful supply of air.   [2]

 iii Name two chemicals that are made when petrol is burned in a reduced supply of air.   [2]

c Larger alkane molecules are often split into smaller ones. What do we call this process?   [1]

d One small molecule that can be produced is ethene. Which of the following is an ethene molecule?   [1]

A	B	C	D
H | H—C—H | H	H H | | H—C—C—H | | H H	H H | | C=C | | H H	H H H | | | H—C—C—C—H | | | H H H
CH_4	C_2H_6	C_2H_4	C_3H_8

e Ethene is used to make polythene. Using the symbol 'E' for ethene, draw a length of the polythene molecule. [1]

[9 marks]

6 Two different fuels are used to heat a beaker of water. The table below shows the results of burning 1 g of each fuel.

a What is the temperature rise at **A**? [1]

Liquid fuel sample	Starting temperature of water (°C)	Final temperature of water (°C)	Temperature change (°C)
Sample 1	20	46	A
Sample 2	23	B	15

b What is the temperature at **B**?   [1]

c What do we call reactions that give out heat?   [1]

d What units are used to measure heat?   [1]

e Scientists are worried that burning fuels will add to the greenhouse effect. What problem is linked with greenhouse gases in the atmosphere?   [1]

[5 marks]

7 A student wanted to see how fast magnesium reacts with hydrochloric acid. She used the same amount of acid and the same mass of magnesium for each experiment.

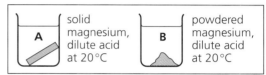

a Use the idea of particles to explain why the reaction in beaker **B** was faster than **A**.   [2]

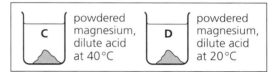

b Use the idea of particles to explain why the reaction in beaker **C** was faster than **D**.   [2]

c Suggest **two** other ways of speeding reactions up.   [2]

[6 marks]

8 Geologists think that a particular type of rock from South America was made from molten magma which came to the surface and quickly cooled.

a What do we call rocks formed when molten magma solidifies?   [1]

b Which of the rocks in the diagram could have cooled quickly? Explain how you can tell.   [1]

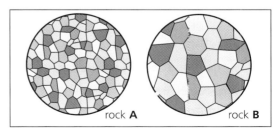

c There is a similar rock in Africa. Geologists think that the two rocks were formed very close to each other. Use ideas about plate tectonics to explain why they are so far apart now. [2]

[4 marks]

9 An archaeologist dug up some buried metal objects.

> • The **Silver** ear-ring was slightly corroded.
> • The **Iron** dagger was very badly corroded.
> • The **Gold** armband was shiny.
> • The **Copper** bracelet was badly corroded.

a Use the information to write the order of reactivity for these metals. Put the **most reactive** metal first. [2]

b Iron does not corrode if the air cannot touch it. What chemical in the air is needed to make the iron corrode? [1]

[3 marks]

10 The flow chart shows how ammonia is made.

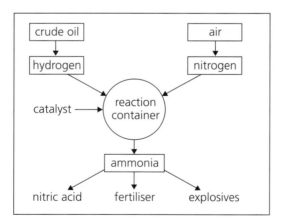

ai Air is a raw material used to make ammonia. Write down the name of the other raw material. [1]

ii Write down **two** uses of ammonia. [2]

iii What are **three** of the costs in making ammonia? [3]

b A catalyst is used in this reaction.

i What is a catalyst? [2]

ii Which catalyst is used in this process? [1]

c The Haber process is a reversible reaction. What is meant by the term 'reversible reaction'? [1]

d The graph shows what percentage of ammonia is produced by the Haber process at different pressures.

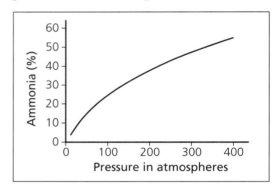

i The plant is usually operated at about 250 atmospheres pressure. What percentage of ammonia should this produce? [1]

ii It is too expensive to build a factory which works at a higher pressure, even though a higher percentage of ammonia would be produced. Suggest one reason why it is more expensive to use a higher pressure. [1]

[12 marks]

11 The nuclear power station at Chernobyl released radioactive dust into the air. Some of the dust fell on the Lake District in Britain. Sheep ate the dust that settled on the grass and produced radioactive milk. Sheep normally use calcium from the grass to make milk, but this time they were using strontium as well.

ai Find strontium in the periodic table of elements and decide how many protons are in the nucleus of a strontium atom. [1]

ii What is the difference between an atom of strontium-88 and an atom of strontium-90? [2]

b Use the periodic table to explain why sheep are likely to take in strontium as well as calcium. [2]

[**5 marks**]

12 Ammonia solution is an alkali. You can make fertiliser by neutralising ammonia solution with an acid. A student investigated neutralisation reactions by adding acid from a burette to alkali in a flask. She measured the pH during the investigation.

ai Suggest a number for pH of the alkali in the flask at the start. [1]

ii Suggest a number for pH of the solution when she had added just enough acid to neutralise the alkali. [1]

iii Suggest a number for pH of the solution if she added one drop too much of the acid. [1]

b Complete the equation:

Acid + alkali = _____ + water [1]

c The fertiliser that she made was ammonium nitrate, $(NH_4)_2NO_3$.

i How many atoms of nitrogen are in the formula of ammonium nitrate? [1]

ii How many different elements are in ammonium nitrate? [1]

iii The relative atomic mass (A_r) of hydrogen (H) is 1.
The relative atomic mass (A_r) of nitrogen (N) is 14.
The relative atomic mass (A_r) of oxygen (O) is 16.

What is the relative formula mass of ammonium nitrate? [1]

d Ammonium nitrate must not be spread on fields if there is likely to be heavy rain. Suggest and explain why not. [2]

[**9 marks**]

13 Use this diagram of the periodic table to help you answer this question.

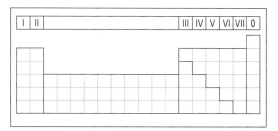

ai Where on the periodic table is the most reactive metal? [2]

ii Where on the periodic table is the most reactive non-metal? [2]

b Use ideas about electron shells to explain why the noble gases (group 0) are not reactive. [1]

c Oxygen has eight electrons and is in group VII.

i How many electrons are in the inner shell of an oxygen atom? [1]

ii How many electrons are in the outer shell of an oxygen atom? [1]

d Magnesium has two electrons in its outer shell. What is the charge on a magnesium ion? [2]

[**9 marks**]

14 Aluminium is produced by the electrolysis of aluminium oxide. Aluminium oxide is made up of Al^{3+} and O^{2-} particles.

a What do we call Al^{3+} and O^{2-} particles? [1]

b Explain why cryolite is used in the process. [1]

c Explain why the molten aluminium oxide will conduct electricity but the solid won't conduct. [1]

d The sides and the bottom of the electrolysis cell are lined with carbon. This is connected to an electricity supply to make the negative electrode. Positive carbon electrodes are dipped into the liquid.

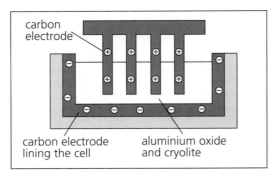

carbon electrode

carbon electrode lining the cell   aluminium oxide and cryolite

i What do we call a positive electrode? [1]

ii What do we call a negative electrode? [1]

iii What happens to the Al^{3+} particles when the current is switched on? [2]
[**7 marks**]

15 We think that wine was first produced by accident when wild yeasts landed on some crushed grapes and made them ferment.

ai What are the **three** important conditions for fermentation to go well? [3]

ii What are the sugars in the grapes converted to during fermentation? [1]

b Yeast contains biological catalysts called enzymes.

i What does a catalyst do to a reaction? [1]

ii What can you say about a catalyst at the end of a reaction? [1]

c Yeast is also used in breadmaking. What does yeast produce to make the bread rise? [1]

d If bread is left in a cold place the yeast will only work very slowly. What will happen to the speed that the yeast works at as the temperature increases? Explain your answer. [4]
[**11 marks**]

16 When petrol burns in air, the carbon inside the petrol turns into carbon dioxide and the small amounts of sulphur inside the petrol turn into a substance which causes acid rain.

ai What substance is formed when sulphur burns in air? [1]

ii Write a word equation for this reaction. [2]

iii Suggest **two** harmful effects of acid rain. [2]

b Large amounts of carbon dioxide are formed when the petrol burns in air.

i This reaction is an example of
**neutralisation precipitation
oxidation reduction** [1]

ii What **name** do we give the environmental problem caused by the carbon dioxide in the atmosphere? [1]

iii What **effect** does too much carbon dioxide have? [1]

iv Carbon dioxide is removed by plants. What carbon compound do the plants convert the carbon dioxide into? [1]

v Sometimes the dead plants do not rot, they form a rock instead. What type of rock is made from the carbon of the dead plants? [1]

vi What is the percentage of carbon dioxide in the atmosphere?
0.04% 0.4% 4% 40% [1]
[**11 marks**]

AT4

Physical Processes

Properties of waves

Jo throws a brick at Sam. The brick (made from matter) transfers some energy from Jo to Sam.

Sam shouts at Jo. He makes a sound wave. The wave transfers some energy to Jo by making the air between them vibrate. There is no transfer of matter from Sam to Jo. Waves can pass through all sorts of things – air, water, rope, springs, and even the Earth (in earthquakes).

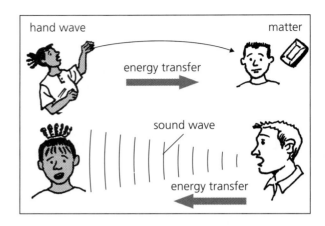

Transverse waves

The easiest type of wave to see is a **transverse wave**. Jo transmits a transverse wave to Sam along a stretched rope by shaking one end of the rope. As the wave travels from left to right, it makes each bit of the rope vibrate up and down. None of the rope from Jo's end travels to Sam's end.

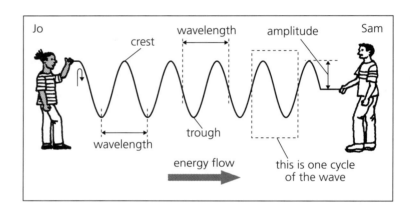

Frequency

The **amplitude** is the height of the wave measured from an invisible central line through the middle of the wave. Amplitude is measured in metres (m).

The **frequency** is the number of cycles made in a second. Frequency is measured in hertz (Hz). The **wavelength** is the distance taken up by each cycle. Wavelength is given in metres (m).

If the frequency increases, the wavelength is shorter so that more cycles can pass through in the same time.

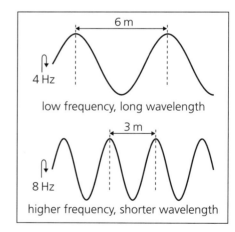

Now do this

1 What is the amplitude of this wave?
2 How many cycles of the wave does this diagram show?
3 What is the wavelength of this wave?

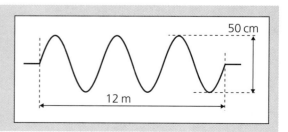

Longitudinal waves

There is another type of wave called a longitudinal wave. This is formed by matter being squeezed and stretched to carry the wave.

You can see this most clearly in a spring.

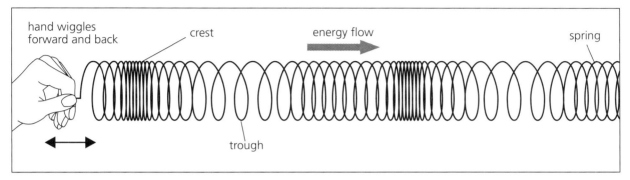

Each coil of the spring is squeezed and stretched in the same direction as the flow of energy.

Sound is a longitudinal wave. It is caused by vibrations which squeeze and stretch the air. The pattern of squeezing and stretching travels through the air as a wave, carrying energy away from the source of the vibrations. When the waves hit your eardrum they make it vibrate and this is how you hear.

The bigger the amplitude of a sound wave the louder the sound you hear. The bigger the frequency, the higher the pitch of the sound you hear.

Now do this

4 Copy and complete the sentences. Choose from the following words:

vibrations   longitudinal   energy flow   frequency   hertz

Sound is created by _____. The number of vibrations per second is the _____ of the wave, measured in _____. Sound is a _____ wave. It makes the air vibrate in the same direction as the _____ _____.

Reflection and refraction

Waves bounce off hard smooth surfaces. This is called **reflection**. Sound waves can be reflected and are heard as an echo.

Light waves

Reflection is vital for us in seeing things. We only see objects when light bounces off them and into our eyes. Light waves travel in straight lines. These can be drawn as rays.

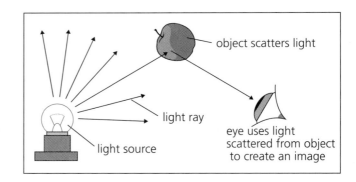

object scatters light

light ray

light source

eye uses light scattered from object to create an image

Light reflects at all angles from most objects which have dull and irregular surfaces, such as a sheet of paper. But when light rays hit a smooth shiny surface like a mirror they reflect back in a regular way. This means that you not only see the mirror but also the image of yourself reflected in the mirror.

The **angle of the reflection** of the light (r) is the same as the angle at which it hits the mirror (known as the **angle of incidence**, i). Both angles are measured from the **normal**. This is an imaginary line at right angles to the mirror.

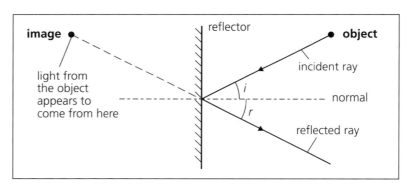

image

reflector

object

light from the object appears to come from here

incident ray

i

normal

r

reflected ray

Light reflected from a flat mirror appears to come from behind the mirror. The distance the image seems to be behind the mirror is the same as the distance from the object to the mirror.

Curved surfaces

Curved mirrors can be used to focus light from a distant object.

Headlamps use curved mirrors to make a beam of light from a lamp.

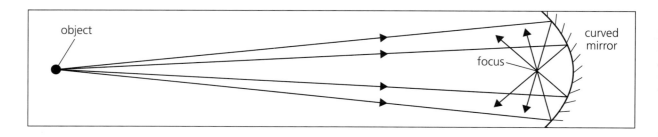

object

focus

curved mirror

Refraction

When light goes from air into water or glass it changes direction. It is **refracted**. Light waves slow down when they enter glass or water. This change of wavelength makes them change direction.

When the light goes into air or water it is always refracted at a smaller angle than the angle of incidence. When it comes out of the material the angle of refraction is always bigger than the angle of incidence. Both angles are measured from the normal.

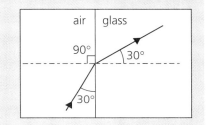
Light passing through a glass prism

Total internal reflection

If the angle of incidence is large enough, rays of light will not refract out. They are reflected back into the glass or water. This is called **total internal reflection**.

Total internal reflection happens in optical fibres. Light going in at one end reflects off the inner edges of the fibre until it gets to the other end. So the image of an object at one end can be seen at the other end.

Optical fibres are used:
- in medicine to look deep inside people's bodies to diagnose problems
- in communication to transmit digital signals rapidly.

Now do this

1 How big are the values of *i* and *r* for this ray of light?

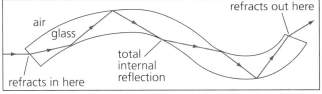

Reflection and refraction in water

Waves on the surface of water are called ripples. Like other waves, ripples can be reflected and refracted. Plane (straight) waves reflect off straight barriers like other waves do. The angle of incidence and the angle of reflection are the same as each other. Ripples move faster in deep water than in shallow water. So ripples are refracted when the water changes depth. The wavelength changes.

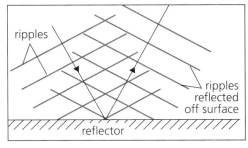

Total internal reflection in an optical fibre

Now do this

2 How is the reflection of straight water ripples off a straight barrier similar to the reflection of light rays off a mirror?

3 When are water waves refracted?

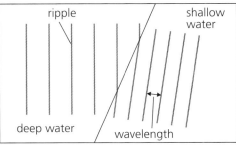

Ultrasound and X-rays

The highest frequency sound that humans can hear is about 20 000 Hz (or 20 kHz). Any sound with higher frequency than 20 kHz is called **ultrasound**.

Now do this

1 Here are the frequencies of five different sound waves. List them in order of increasing frequency. Which of them will be ultrasound?

   12 000 Hz   24 kHz   47 Hz   50 000 Hz   900 Hz.

Measuring distance

Ships use pulses of ultrasound to find out what is underneath them. Each pulse reflects off solid objects in the water. A microphone under the ship listens for these echoes. The time between the pulse and its echo is used to calculate the distance from the ship to whatever has reflected the pulse. This is called **sonar**.

Ultrasound is used in industry to clean small objects, such as rings. The object hangs in water and ultrasound vibrates the dirt loose.

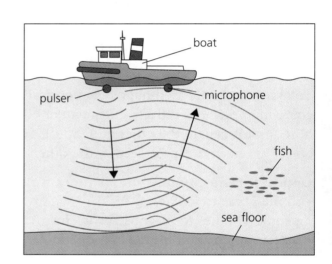

Using ultrasound in medicine

Ultrasound is used to look inside the human body. Pulses of ultrasound go through the skin. Each time a pulse passes from one organ into another, some of it is reflected back to the skin. These echoes can be used to form a picture of what is under the skin without the need for surgery. Ultrasound is often used to scan babies before they are born.

Kidney stones can be shaken into small pieces by ultrasound. This avoids the need for surgery to cut the patient open to remove the stones.

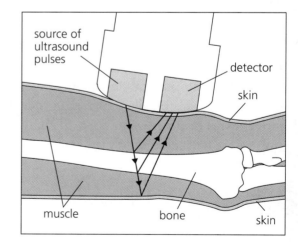

Now do this

2 Describe two different uses of ultrasound in medicine.

Electromagnetic waves

The electromagnetic spectrum is a family or group of waves which all travel at the speed of light. The light we see (**visible light**) is part of this family. These waves all have different wavelengths and they are listed here in order of the size of their wavelengths.

radio	microwaves	infra-red	visible light	ultra-violet	X-rays	gamma-rays
longest wavelength					shortest wavelength	

Radio waves are used to carry sound and pictures (for example, radio and TV).

Microwaves are used to communicate with satellites in space. If they have the right wavelength they are absorbed by water and heat it up, so can be used to cook food. This also means that they can cause burns if absorbed by body tissue.

Infra-red waves heat up any object which absorbs them. They are given out by hot objects, such as electric fires. They also carry information as data pulses down optical fibres. Infra-red cameras which detect anything warmer than their surroundings can also be used for night time photography. The greatest danger from infra-red radiation is burns.

Ultra-violet waves damage living cells and can cause skin cancer. They are given out by the Sun and also by fluorescent lights. Dark skin will absorb ultra-violet waves and protect the living cells underneath.

X-rays pass through flesh but are absorbed by bone. They allow photographs to be made of bones. X-rays can also kill living cells and can cause cancer.

Gamma-rays can pass through steel and concrete. They are very dangerous, but can be used to detect and destroy cancer cells. Special precautions are needed for those who use X-rays or gamma-rays in their jobs.

The longer the wavelength, the lower the frequency so all parts of the electromagnetic spectrum have different frequencies as well.

Electromagnetic waves in our living room

Now do this

3 Which parts of the electromagnetic spectrum:
a are used for communication?
b are dangerous to living cells?
c can be used for heating food?
d are used to transmit TV pictures?

Heat energy transfer

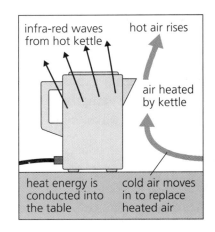

infra-red waves from hot kettle

hot air rises

air heated by kettle

heat energy is conducted into the table

cold air moves in to replace heated air

If you boil a kettle and then leave it, it eventually cools down to room temperature. Why does this happen? The answer is that heat energy flows from the hot kettle to the cold room until they are both at the same temperature.

There are three ways in which the kettle loses its heat energy:
- by **conduction** through the base of the table
- by **convection** as hot air rises from the sides
- by **radiation** as infra-red waves carry energy away.

Now do this

1   A mug of coffee at 40 °C is placed in a freezer at –20 °C.
   a What will the final temperature of the mug be?
   b What are the three ways in which the heat energy leaves the mug?

Conduction

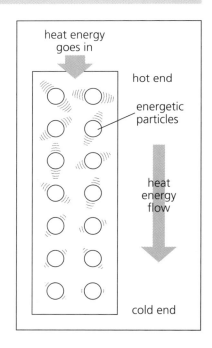

heat energy goes in

hot end

energetic particles

heat energy flow

cold end

The heat energy of the kettle is the movement (**kinetic**) energy of its particles. The particles in the solid kettle walls are always moving. They vibrate and the faster they vibrate the hotter the kettle is.

The movement of the particles leads to heat energy being conducted through solids. When one end of a solid is hotter than the other, the energy of the particles at the hot end is passed on to other particles right the way up to the cold end. The heat energy is conducted.

In an electric kettle the heat is conducted from the heating element to the water, from the water to the sides and bottom of the kettle and from the bottom of the kettle to the table on which it stands.

Now do this

2   Copy and complete these sentences. Choose from the following words:

kinetic   conduction   energy   vibrate

Particles in a solid have _____ energy which makes them _____.
Particles in a hot solid have more _____ than particles in a cold solid.
The process of heat transfer through a solid is called _____.

Convection

Air particles which hit the hot surface of the kettle also gain extra kinetic energy. So the air around the kettle heats up. The warm air expands and gets lighter so that it rises up, carrying the extra heat energy with it. The heat energy is **convected** upwards.

Cold air, which is heavier, flows in to take the place of the hot air. This too heats up and rises as well. In this way **convection currents** are set up around the kettle.

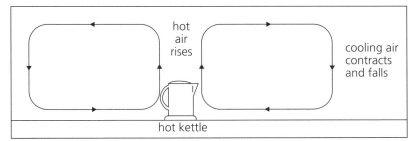

Evaporation

Liquids can also lose heat energy by evaporation. Particles at the surface of a liquid escape if they have enough energy. So the particles with the most energy gradually leave the liquid. Only the less energetic particles are left behind, leaving a colder liquid.

 Now do this

3   The cooling element of a fridge is always at the top.
 a What happens to the air particles when they hit the element?
 b Describe the convection currents inside the fridge.

4   Convection currents are set up in liquids too. The electric kettle has a water heater at the bottom. Describe the convection currents in the water which ensure that all the water is boiled.

Radiation

Like all hot objects, the surface of the kettle emits infra-red radiation. Black surfaces are much better at radiating heat than shiny ones. So a shiny kettle will lose heat energy less rapidly than a coloured one.

Shiny objects reflect infra-red rays, so they heat up slowly. Black objects absorb infra-red rays, so they heat up quickly.

 Now do this

5   Copy and complete the sentences with the words **Good** or **Bad**.

Silver objects are _____ radiators and _____ absorbers of heat radiation.
Black objects are _____ radiators and _____ absorbers of heat radiation.

6   What happens to a liquid as the energy of its particles gets less?

7   How can evaporation cool down a liquid?

Saving energy

Heating your home

There are two ways of heating a home. You can use electricity or burn a fuel, such as wood, coal, oil or gas. If you use electricity you have electric heaters in each room. These heat the air by convection and radiation.

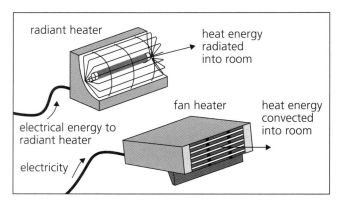

If you use coal or wood, you could burn it in each room but you are more likely to use fuels in a central heating system. Here you burn the fuel to heat water or air which is then carried to each room in the home by pipes or air ducts.

Installing the pipes or ducts is expensive. It is often cheaper to put an electrical heater in each room. But electricity itself is expensive so its running costs are greater.

Burning fuels also produces waste gases which can pollute the environment. Making electricity also often causes pollution, but it is easier to control this at the power station.

You can also use electricity or fossil fuels, especially gas, for cooking. The cost of buying an electric cooker and a gas cooker is very similar.

You can read more about fossil fuels on pages 23 and 61.

Now do this

1 Give **two** reasons for using electrical heaters for heating.

2 Give **two** reasons for using fossil fuels for heating.

Using the Earth's resources

Coal, oil and gas are **non-renewable** fuels. Once they are used up, they are gone forever. We will then have to use **renewable** energy sources.

Renewable sources of electricity include:

- energy from the Sun (solar energy), using solar cells
- wind energy using wind turbines
- tidal energy in the sea, using dams across estuaries
- trees – convert the Sun's energy into chemical energy
- hydroelectric energy, using the energy of falling water in the mountains.

Now do this

3 Name **one** renewable fuel for heating a home.

4 Name **five** renewable sources of electricity.

Saving energy at home

Heating a building can be expensive. You can cut down fuel or electricity bills by using **insulation**.

Some of this insulation can be built into a house when you install:
- double glazing, which is two sheets of glass at a window, with air between them
- roof insulation
- wall insulation.

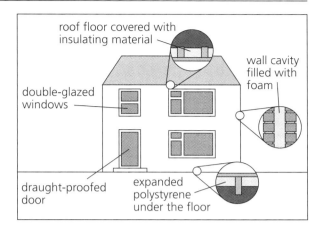

You can also cut down heat loss through windows by using curtains. These also provide insulation.

How does insulation work?

Many good insulators contain air. Heat does not pass very easily though air. Double glazing traps air between two panes of glass. Roof insulation and curtains trap air in tiny pockets within the materials.

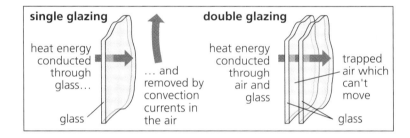

Insulators are the opposite of conductors. Metals are good conductors. Heat energy flows quickly through them. This is why saucepans are metal.

How much can you save?

It costs a lot to double-glaze the windows in a house. How many years does it take before the double-glazing pays for itself?

Example: It costs £5000 to double-glaze all the windows in a house and this cuts the annual heating bill from £750 to £500.

So it takes 20 years to pay back the cost of the double glazing. This is called the **pay-back** time.

The money saved in a year
= £750 − £500 = £250
£5000 (the set-up cost)
divided by £250 = 20.

Now do this

5 The annual cost of heating a house drops from £800 to £600 when £1000 is spent on insulation in the roof and walls. Calculate the pay-back time.

6 Complete the sentences.

Wool is an _____ because it contains trapped _____. Copper is a _____ because it is a _____.

Mains electricity

Working out the cost

Every electrical appliance has a voltage and power rating. The voltage rating is usually 230 V in Europe. The power is measured in watts (W) or kilowatts (kW).

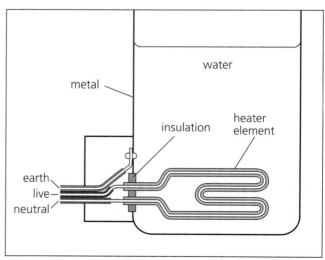

250 W microwave oven

3 kW heater

The power rating of an appliance can be used to calculate how much electrical energy it will use. You multiply it by the number of hours the appliance is switched on.

1 kW = 1000 W

One kilowatt-hour (kWh) of energy is called a **unit of electricity**. It costs about 10 pence. Off-peak electricity at night costs less.

energy (kilowatt-hour) = power (kilowatt) × time (hour)

Example: An electric fire has a power of 1 kW. If a unit of electricity costs 10 p, calculate the cost of running the fire for 5 hours.

Units (kWh) used $= 1 \times 5$
$\qquad = 5 \, kWh$
cost $=$ units $\times 10 = 5 \times 10$
$\qquad = 50 \, p$

Now do this

1 If an off-peak unit of electricity costs 6 p, calculate how much it costs to run a 2.5 kW water heater for 4 hours at night.

2 An electric cooker has four 1 kW heating rings, a 1.5 kW grill and a 2 kW oven. Calculate how much it costs to use all the cooker elements for half an hour. A unit of electricity costs 10 p.

Safe wiring

Electrical appliances are connected to the 230 V mains supply by a pair of metal wires. They are called **live** and **neutral**. If the appliance has a metal outside case, there will be a third **earth** wire as well.

Each wire has a different coloured covering (insulation). The insulation is important to stop people being electrocuted by the live wire. But insulation is also important to keep the wires apart otherwise the current may

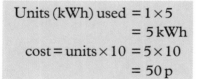

water

metal

insulation

heater element

earth
live
neutral

Electrical connections to a water heater

take a short cut through the wires and not run through the appliance. For the same reason it is important that the connections in a plug at the ends of the wires are kept well apart.

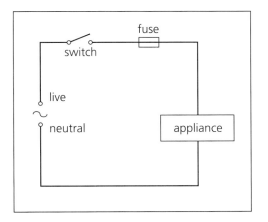

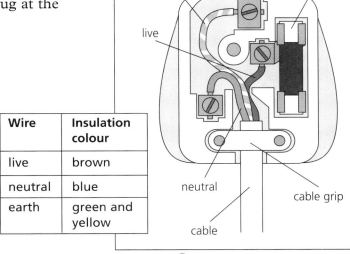

Wire	Insulation colour
live	brown
neutral	blue
earth	green and yellow

The live wire carries the energy from the supply to the appliance. The neutral wire completes the circuit for the electric current.

Fuses

There should be a fuse in the live wire. This switches off the current if it gets too high. Large currents in a wire can cause it to get hot and damage its insulation. The fuse is the thinnest wire in the circuit, so it melts (blows) first, before the other wires are damaged. **Circuit breakers** are also used. These can be reset more easily than fuses.

Earthing appliances

The earth wire should always be connected to the metal outside of an appliance. Then if the live wire comes loose and touches the outside, the current flows safely away through the earth wire.

Appliances which are double insulated do not need an earth wire. If the live wire comes loose, it can't touch any metal which is on the outside of the appliance.

Now do this

3 a Name the three wires connecting an electrical heater to the mains supply.
b What colour is the insulation of each one?

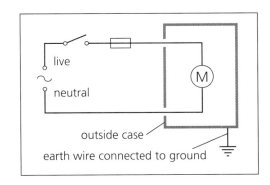

Now do this

4 Explain how a fuse protects the insulation of mains wires.
5 Where should the earth wire be connected to an appliance? Why?
6 What type of appliance does not need an earth wire?

Measuring motion

Measuring speed

Jo's car has a top speed of 35 metres per second (m/s). This means that it can move forwards 35 metres in each second. Or 70 metres in two seconds. You can work out its speed by using this formula. (You must know this one by heart!).

$$speed = \frac{distance}{time}$$

The distance and time must be measured in metres(m) and seconds(s) for the answer to be in metres per second (m/s).

Example:

A car travels 1.2 km in a minute.
Calculate its speed in metres per second.

distance = 1.2 km = 1200 m
time = 1 minute = 60 s
speed = $\frac{1200}{60}$
= 20 m/s

Always put the distance and time into the correct units before you calculate the speed!

 Now do this

1 A car travels 400 m in 20 s. Calculate its speed.

2 Sound can travel 1.2 km in 4 s. How fast does it move?

3 Bill can walk 0.5 km in 5 minutes. How fast can he walk?

4 The legal top speed for a car is 110 km per hour. What is this in m/s?

If you say which direction an object is moving in as well as its speed, you are giving its velocity. The velocity of a car might be 25 m/s north. The velocity of a rocket might be 50 m/s upwards.

Distance–time graphs

Distance–time graphs are a very good way of describing motion.

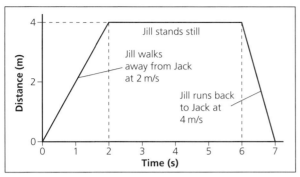

Jill stands still

Jill walks away from Jack at 2 m/s

Jill runs back to Jack at 4 m/s

Now do this

5 Sam walks away from Jo at 1 m/s for 5 s. He then stops for 10 s. Draw a distance-time graph for Sam.

Here is a distance-time graph for Paul. He walks away slowly, stops for a while and then runs away quickly.

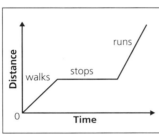

This can also be shown in a speed–time (or velocity–time) graph.

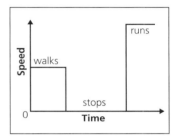

Now do this

6 Here are three speed–time graphs. Match each one with a sentence from this list.
a Speeding up to a steady speed. **b** Moving at a steady speed.
c Moving at a steady speed and then slowing to a halt.

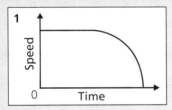

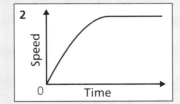

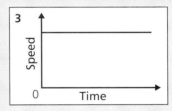

Here is a speed-time graph for Jake as he goes from rest to top speed on his bike. The distance travelled is equal to the area under the line.

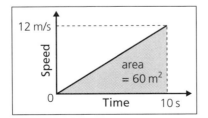

area = 60 m²

The area is triangular in shape, with a base of 10 s and a height of 12 m/s.

Now do this

7 A car slows from 30 m/s to 0 m/s in 5 s.
a Draw a speed-time graph for the car as it slows down.
b Use the graph to work out how far the car travels.

$$\text{distance} = \tfrac{1}{2}\,\text{base} \times \text{height} = 0.5 \times 10 \times 12 = 60 \text{ m}^2$$

Speeding up and slowing down

Acceleration

If you start to go faster on your bike or in a car you are **accelerating**. Your speed increases as time goes on.

Here is the speed–time graph for a bike which is accelerating.

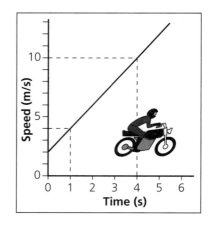

The speed increases from 4 metres a second (m/s) to 10 m/s, a change of 6 m/s. It takes 3 seconds to do this. So the speed changes by 2 m/s each second. The bike accelerates at 2 m/s^2 (metres per second squared).

Here is the formula for calculating acceleration. You need to know it by heart!

$$\text{acceleration} = \frac{\text{change of speed}}{\text{time taken}}$$

 Now do this

1 Write down the formula for calculating acceleration.

2 What are the units of acceleration?

3 A plane takes 4 s to get from a speed of 5 m/s to 45 m/s. Calculate its acceleration.

Friction

Jo pedals her bike along a level road. She stops pedalling. The force of **friction** slows her down until she stops.

Friction is measured in newtons (N).

The friction comes from
- the air in front of the bike which is pushed aside
- the contact between the tyres and the road
- the moving parts of the bike rubbing past each other.

The acceleration of the bike depends on the size of Jo's thrust compared with the friction.

Forces on the bike	Motion of the bike
thrust greater than friction	speed increases
thrust and friction the same	speed doesn't change
thrust smaller than friction	speed decreases

 Now do this

4 State the sources of friction on a moving car.

5 Say whether these objects are speeding up, slowing down or moving at a steady speed.

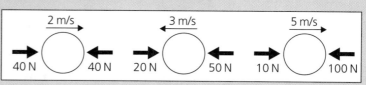

Mass and acceleration

Lighter objects accelerate more quickly than heavier ones when subjected to the same force. So a heavy lorry accelerates far more slowly than a small car when the same amount of force is applied to it.

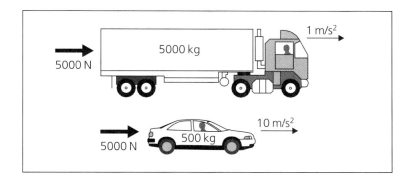

 Now do this

6 An empty van has a larger acceleration than a full one. Why?

Stopping safely

Sam is driving along the road at a steady speed. He sees a tree across the road ahead of him. He brakes and stops. Here are speed–time and distance–time graphs for the car as it slows down.

The **thinking distance** is how far the car travels between Sam noticing the tree and the brakes starting to slow down the car.

It will increase if:
• Sam is not concentrating
• he is tired
• he has been drinking alcohol.

The **braking distance** is how far the car travels once the brakes have started to slow it down. It will increase if:
• the brakes are not adjusted correctly which reduces their friction on the wheel
• the road surface is wet or loose which reduces friction from the road
• the tyres are inflated wrongly
• the tyres don't have enough tread which reduces their friction on the road.

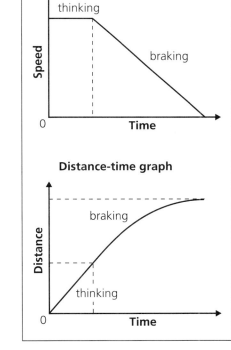

The gap between cars on the road needs to be more than the thinking distance, otherwise they will collide when the one in front stops suddenly. Ouch!

 Now do this

7 Explain what the thinking distance is. What increases thinking distance?

8 Explain what the breaking distance is. What increases braking distance?

Stretching and squeezing

Clare stretches a rubber band. When she lets go of the band it returns to its original shape. This is because rubber is an **elastic** material.

Sam does the same experiment with a polythene bag. When he lets go of it, the bag stays stretched. Polythene is an **inelastic** material.

Now do this

1   Copy and complete these sentences using words from this list:

   inelastic   elastic   length   force   smaller   longer

   When a _____ is applied to an object its _____ changes. If the object is stretched, its length gets _____. If the object is _____, it returns to its original length when the force is removed. If the object is _____, its length doesn't change when the _____ is removed.

If you stretch **elastic** materials hard enough you will reach a point where they break or stay permanently out of shape. A rubber band will break if you stretch it hard enough. A metal spring is less likely to break but it will stay stretched after a certain point instead of bouncing back.

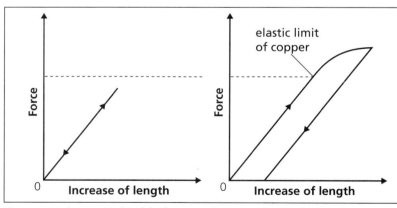

Copper wire stretched below and above its elastic limit

Car safety

Inelastic materials are good at absorbing energy in car crashes. The movement energy of the car squashes the metal in the 'crumple zone' instead of squashing the driver. The crumpled metal does not bounce back but stays deformed.

energy absorbed in crumple

seat belt slows driver down slowly

Seat belts are made of an elastic material but they become inelastic if stretched enough. In a crash the driver is thrown forward and the seat belt holds him or her in place. The kinetic energy of the driver permanently stretches the belt so it should always be replaced after a bad crash.

Many cars now have air bags which expand rapidly in a collision. Car air bags fill rapidly with gas in a collision. Gases can be easily squashed so the bag provides a soft, flat surface which cushions the driver's head as it is thrown forward.

 ## Now do this

2   Describe three safety features of a car which can protect the driver in a collision. Explain how they provide protection.

Under pressure

The pressure which is applied in a car crash can be calculated with this formula. (You need to know it!)

pressure = $\dfrac{\text{force}}{\text{area}}$ or $P = \dfrac{F}{A}$

Symbol	Meaning	Units of measurement
P	pressure	pascals or Pa
F	force	newtons or N
A	area	metres squared or m^2

Now do this

1. Write down the formula for calculating pressure.
2. Write down the units for force, area and pressure.
3. What is the formula for pressure using symbols? What do the symbols mean?

Example: A concrete block sits on the ground. The block weighs 5000 N. The base of the block is 0.5 m by 0.5 m. What is the pressure on the ground under the block?

$P = ?$
$F = 5000\,\text{N}$
$A = 0.5\,\text{m} \times 0.5\,\text{m} = 0.25\,\text{m}^2$

$P = \dfrac{F}{A} = \dfrac{5000}{0.25} = 20\,000\,\text{Pa}$

Now do this

4. The base of a 2000 N block is 0.2 m by 0.2 m.
   Calculate the pressure on the ground under the block.

The importance of area

If a paving slab lies flat on the ground it will apply less pressure on the ground than if it stands on its edge. So, for example, a slab 0.5 m by 0.8 m by 0.05 m can be placed on the ground in three different ways.

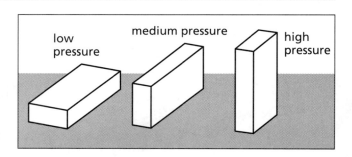

It weighs 400 N. When it is flat on the ground, the area of contact is 0.5 m × 0.8 m = 0.4 m^2.
So the pressure is 400 N/0.4 m^2 = 1000 Pa.

Now do this

5. Calculate the pressure of the slab when it is placed on its smallest edge.

Large forces on small areas can damage surfaces. Think about pushing on a drawing pin!

The pressure can be kept down to a safe level by making the area of contact with a surface large enough.

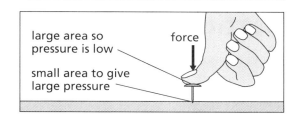

large area so pressure is low

small area to give large pressure

force

Now do this

6   Copy and complete these sentences with the words **pressure, force** and **area**.

A tractor has large tyres. This allows the _____ of the tractor to be applied over a large _____ giving a low _____ on the ground. The wheels sink into the ground if the _____ is too big.

Pressure in liquids

Pressure can be transmitted through liquids. Liquids transmit pressure equally in all directions. This can be very useful.

In car brakes, the driver's foot presses on the brake pedal. This pushes a piston (the master piston) down into the brake fluid. The fluid presses on the slave pistons behind the brake pads and these force the pads against the wheel. So when the brake pedal is pushed, the brake pads are forced against the brake drum.

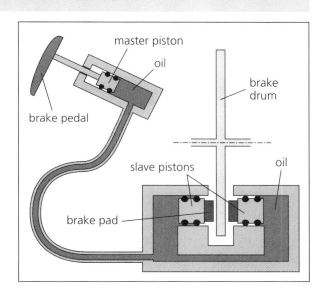

master piston

oil

brake drum

brake pedal

slave pistons

oil

brake pad

Example

A brake force of 50 N is applied to the master piston of area 0.001 m². This puts a pressure of 50/0.001 = 50 000 Pa on the brake fluid.

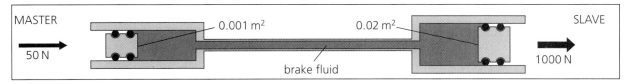

MASTER

0.001 m²

0.02 m²

SLAVE

50 N

brake fluid

1000 N

The pressure at the slave piston will also be 50 000 Pa. Its area is 0.02 m², so the force on the brake pads is 50 000 × 0.02 = 1000 N.

Now do this

7   A force of 100 N is applied to a master piston of area 0.004 m². The slave piston has area 0.1 m². Calculate the force on the slave piston.

Static electricity

Jo walks across the room. Her feet rub against the carpet, pulling tiny particles (**electrons**) off it. As the number of electrons on her builds up, Jo becomes charged with **static electricity**.

electrons transferred from carpet to Jo

carpet

electrons move quickly from Jo to handle

When Jo reaches the door, she touches the metal handle. All the electrons which she knocked off the carpet flow rapidly through her into the metal handle. She loses the charge but gets an electric shock at the same time.

Materials which allow electrons to move through them are conductors. Things which electrons cannot move through are insulators. Metals and water are conductors. Most other materials (such as glass, wood and plastic) are insulators. Static electricity only builds up on insulators as the charge connot flow away through the material.

Positive and negative charge

There are two sorts of charge, positive and negative. Electrons have a negative charge so the material which collects them is negatively charged. The material which loses the electrons has lost some of its negative charge so it is positively charged.

The sort of charge picked up by objects when they are rubbed against each other depends on the two materials involved.

 Now do this

1   Copy and complete these sentences using the following words:

**charged   electrons
comb   insulator**

A nylon comb is an _____. When it passes through hair, _____ are pulled off the hair and carried away by the _____. This leaves the comb _____.

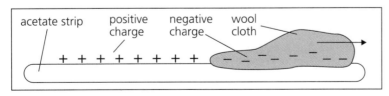

acetate strip   positive charge   negative charge   wool cloth

For example, polythene becomes negative when rubbed with wool – the wool becomes positive. Acetate becomes positive when rubbed with wool – the wool becomes negative.

 Now do this

2   Fur becomes positive when rubbed on glass. What happens to the glass?

Attracting and repelling

- Objects with any charge attract objects with no charge.
- Objects with the same charge always repel each other.
- Objects with different charges always attract each other.

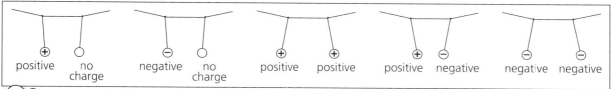

 ## Now do this

3　The table shows the effect of bringing object L close to object R. Complete the table with the words attract or repel.

Charge on L	Charge on R	Effect
positive	negative	
positive	none	
negative	negative	

Using electrostatic forces

Photocopiers and laser printers use static electricity. Reflected light from a document coats an insulating surface with a pattern of positive charge. This attracts particles of negatively charged toner. The pattern of toner is transferred to strongly positively charged paper. The toner is fixed to the paper by heating to create a copy.

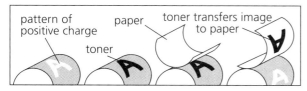

Electrostatic charge can be used to remove ash from the waste gases in coal burning power stations.

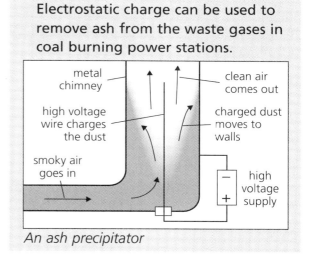

An ash precipitator

Dangers of electrostatic forces

Airplanes in flight become charged as they move rapidly through the air. The charge must be removed safely when the aircraft lands. Otherwise, there may be a spark between the airplane and the metal nozzle of the refuelling pipe. The spark (which is a rapid flow of electrons through the air) could ignite the fuel.

 ## Now do this

4　Name two devices which use static electricity.

5　Suggest why you can get an electric shock when you touch the body of a car after a journey.

The picture on a television screen is made by firing electrons on the screen. This gives it negative charge (static), so it attracts dust in the room.

Measuring electricity

Circuits

Here is the circuit diagram for a lamp connected to a battery by a pair of wires. A battery is made of several cells.

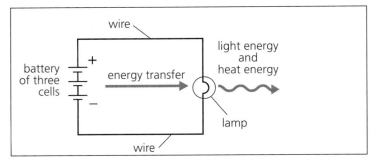

Chemical energy in a battery makes electrons in the metal wires of the circuit flow from the negative terminal (−) to the positive one (+). A flow of electrons or **charge** is called a **current**. There is only a current if the circuit is complete and unbroken.

Voltage

All electrical components have a **voltage rating**. This should be the same as the voltage of the power supply. If components are wired in parallel they all receive the full voltage.

In gases and some solutions a current is a flow of both positive and negative particles, e.g. in electrolysis.

If you put components in series with each other, they share the supply voltage between them.

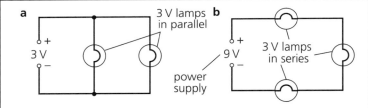

The voltage across a component is measured by connecting a voltmeter in parallel with it. Voltage is measured in volts (or V).

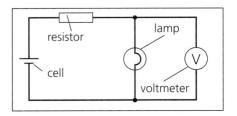

Electrical energy (or electricity) is converted into:

- heat and light energy by lamps
- kinetic energy by motors
- heat energy by resistors
- sound energy by bells and buzzers
- light energy by LEDs.

Now do this

1 Copy and complete these sentences Choose from the following:

series   6   battery   parallel

A 6 V lamp should be connected in _____ with a single _____ V battery.

Four 3 V motors should be connected in _____ with a single 12 V _____.

Measuring current

Current is measured in amps (or A). It has the same value all the way round a series circuit. In a parallel circuit the current drawn from the electricity supply is the sum of the currents in all the components.

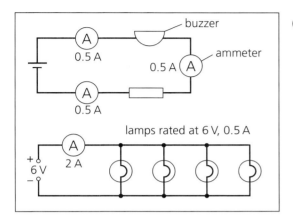

The amount of current in a component is measured with an ammeter. The meter is connected in series with the components.

 Now do this

2 Fill in the readings of the ammeters in this circuit.

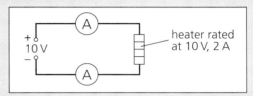

3 One lamp draws a current of 0.25 A when connected to a supply. How much current will be drawn by 8 bulbs connected in parallel to the same supply?

Types of current

There are two types of current. Sources of **direct current** (**dc**) have the same direction of current all the time. Batteries and solar cells supply dc. Sources of **alternating current** (**ac**) keep changing the direction of the current. Dynamos and generators supply ac.

Calculating power

You can work out the power of an electrical component using this formula:

power = current × voltage $P = I \times V$

Symbol	Meaning	Units of measurement
P	power	joules/s or watts (W)
V	voltage	volts or V
I	current	amps or A

Example

There is a current of 2 A in an electric drill connected to 230 V. Calculate the power of the drill.

$P = I \times V$

$P = 2 \times 230 = 460\,\text{W}$

 Now do this

4 There is a current of 5 A in a lamp connected to a 12 V battery. Calculate the power of the lamp.

5 Find the symbols for the following on this page and copy them down: cell, power supply, lamp, ammeter, voltmeter, motor, heater.

Resistance

All electrical components have **resistance**. This means that they resist the current in them. Different components have different levels of resistance.

A big resistance means a small current. So two bulbs in series have a larger resistance than just one on its own.

Components can have the same voltage but different currents. If a 3 V motor has a smaller resistance than a 3 V bulb, then it has a larger current. As the voltage of a component increases, so does the current.

Some resistors are variable. You can use them to control the current in a circuit by changing their resistance. A **rheostat** is a **variable resistor**.

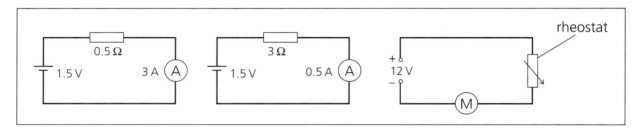

Now do this

1 Which of these circuits has the highest resistance?

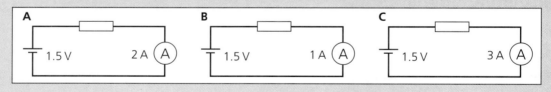

You can work out the resistance of an electrical component with this formula.

$$\text{resistance} = \frac{\text{voltage}}{\text{current}} \qquad R = \frac{V}{I}$$

Symbol	Meaning	Units of measurement
R	resistance	ohms or Ω
V	voltage	volts or V
I	current	amps or A

Now do this

2 Write down the formula for electrical resistance in words.

3 Write down the symbols and units for resistance, voltage and current.

4 Write down the formula for resistance using symbols.

Example

There is a current of 0.2 A in a resistor connected to a 3.0 V battery. Calculate the resistance.

$R = ?$
$V = 3.0 \text{ V}$
$I = 0.2 \text{ A}$

$$R = \frac{V}{I} = \frac{3.0}{0.2} = 15 \; \Omega$$

Now do this

5 A resistor passes a current of 0.5 A when the voltage across it is 24 V. Calculate its resistance.

Voltage-current curves

These graphs show how the current in a wire resistor and a lamp depend on the voltage across them. Their graphs look exactly the same if the voltage is reversed.

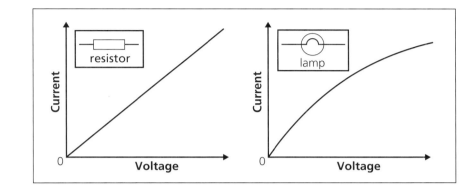

Diodes

The resistance of a **diode** depends on the voltage across it. The current rises steeply when the anode voltage rises above the cathode voltage.

An **LED** (light emitting diode) is a special diode which emits light.

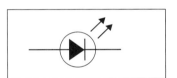

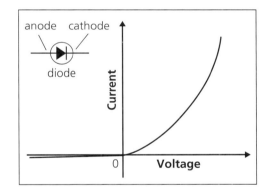

A **thermistor** can be used to turn off the heating when the temperature gets high enough. The resistance of a thermistor depends on its temperature. A suitable electronic circuit can use this resistance change to turn the heater on and off.

A similar system uses an LDR (light dependent resistor) to control lights. The resistance of an LDR depends on the amount of light hitting it. A lot of money can be saved by switching off the lights automatically.

Now do this

6 Sketch graphs to show how the current depends on the voltage for a resistor and a lamp.

7 Sketch a voltage-current graph for a diode.

Now do this

8 Name a component which detects temperature.

9 Name a component which detects light.

Energy at work

Calculating work

Jo lifts up a brick from the floor. She puts it on the table. This increases the **gravitational potential energy** (or **PE**) of the brick. This energy comes from Jo.

work = force × distance
$W = F \times d$

The **work** done by Jo equals the PE gained by the brick. The amount of work she did can be calculated by multiplying the force she used to move the brick by the distance she moved the brick. Work is the same as the amount of energy transferred. Like all forms of energy, it is measured in joules.

Symbol	Meaning	Units of measurement
W	work	joules or J
F	force	newtons or N
d	distance	metres or m

 Now do this

1 Write down the formula for work in words.

2 Write down the symbols and units for work, force and distance.

3 Write down the formula for work using symbols.

Example

Sam moves a table across the floor, pushing with a force of 20 N. How much work does he do if the table moves 4 m?

$W = F \times d$
$W = 20 \times 4 = 80$ **J**

Kinetic energy

Moving objects have **kinetic energy** (or **KE**). The faster they go, the more KE they have. Like PE, KE is measured in joules.

 Now do this

4 A brick weighs 25 N. Calculate the work needed to raise a brick by 3 m. How much PE does the brick gain in the process?

Sam does work on Jo

Jo gains kinetic energy

 Now do this

5 Jo applies a force of 50 N to her bike. It moves forwards on level ground. How much KE has it gained after moving 10 m?

The heavier a moving object is, the more kinetic energy it has.

Turning PE into KE

Sam throws a ball of clay into the air. As it rises, it turns its KE into PE. The clay has maximum PE at the top of its flight. On the way down again, the PE turns back into KE. When the clay lands on the ground, all of the KE that Sam gave it becomes heat energy.

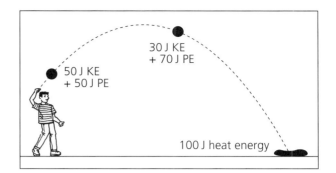

30 J KE + 70 J PE

50 J KE + 50 J PE

100 J heat energy

 ## Now do this

6 Copy and complete these sentences. Choose from the following words:

potential   kinetic   heat   chemical   potential

Sally climbs up the ladder of a slide, turning _____ energy into _____ energy. As she slides down, she turns _____ energy into _____ energy. As she slides to a halt at the end, all of the KE has become _____ energy.

Measuring power

The **power** of a machine tells you how much work it can do in a second. A motor with a high power can deliver energy more quickly than one with a low power. So cars with high power engines can accelerate and climb up hills faster than cars with low power engines.

$$\text{power} = \frac{\text{work}}{\text{time}} \qquad P = \frac{W}{T}$$

Symbol	Meaning	Units of measurement
P	power	watts or W
W	work	joules or J
t	time	seconds or S

 ## Now do this

7 Write down the formula for power in words.

8 Write down the symbols and units for power, work and time.

9 Write down the formula for power using symbols.

Example

Rollin does 2000 J of work lifting bricks up a building. This takes him 50 s. Calculate his power.

$P = ?$
$W = 2000\,J$ $\quad P = \frac{2000}{50} = 40\,W$
$t = 50\,s$

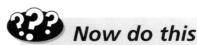 ## Now do this

10 A crane does 1600 J of work in 8 s. Calculate its power.

Magnetism

Magnets attract iron and steel which has not been magnetised. They ignore all other metals except cobalt and nickel.

The end of a magnet is called its **pole**. One pole is called south (S) and the other end is north (N). Either pole of a magnet will attract unmagnetised iron.
Poles which are the same always repel each other.
Poles which are different always attract each other.

Now do this

1   Here are some pairs of objects. For each pair, do they repel, attract or ignore each other?

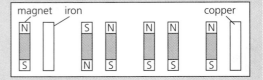

Magnetic fields

Here is the **magnetic field** around a bar magnet. Each **field line** has an arrow on it. The field lines tell you which way the needle of a compass points.

Now do this

2   Name the four materials which are attracted to magnets.

3   Name the pole at T on this magnet.

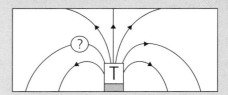

4   Which way will the compass needle point?

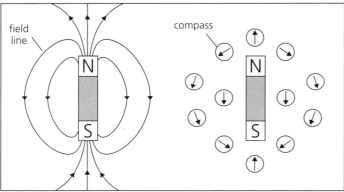

The field lines come out of the north pole of the magnet and return at the south pole of the magnet. These are the field lines of magnets which are attracting and repelling each other.

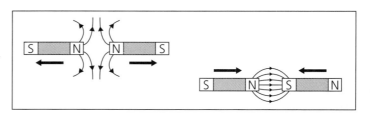

Current and magnets

There is a force on a conductor (such as copper) which carries an electric current in a magnetic field.

The force is at right angles to both the current and the field. The direction of the force can be reversed by reversing the direction of either the current or the field.

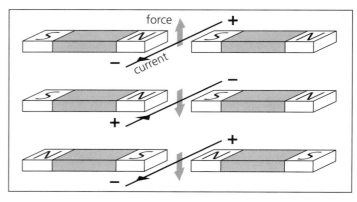

Generating electricity

Electricity can be generated by moving a wire through a magnetic field. The voltage changes sign if the wire is moved the other way.

The size of the voltage can be increased by speeding up the movement of the wire and increasing the strength of the field.

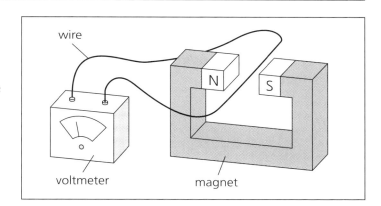

wire

N S

voltmeter   magnet

Now do this

5   The voltmeter reads + 0.1 V as the wire is pulled up through the poles of the magnet. What will it read when the wire is
   a pushed down
   b held still between the poles of the magnet?

6   What two things could you do to increase the reading of the voltmeter in Q5?

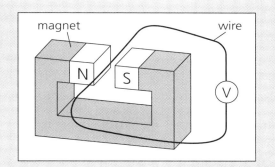

magnet   wire

N S

V

Electricity is generated on a large scale by spinning large coils of copper wire inside the fields of large magnets. The alternating current in the coil is brought out of the generator by brushes pressing on slip rings.

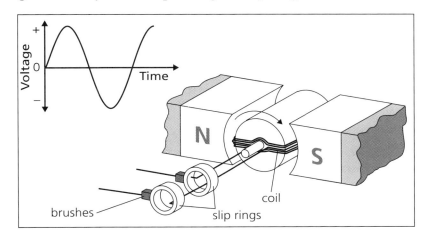

Voltage
+
0
Time
−

N S

brushes
slip rings
coil

You can read about generating electricity on pages 130 and 131.

Now do this

7   A generator always contains lots of steel and copper. Suggest what each material is used for in the generator.

Electromagnets in action

There is a magnetic field around a coil of insulated wire carrying an electric current.

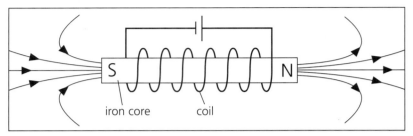

iron core   coil

A U-shaped **electromagnet** is used to pick up iron objects. It only attracts them when the current in the coil is switched on. The U-shaped core is made of soft iron to increase the strength of the coil's magnetism.

An electromagnet becomes stronger if:
• more coils of wire are put on it
• the current in it is increased.

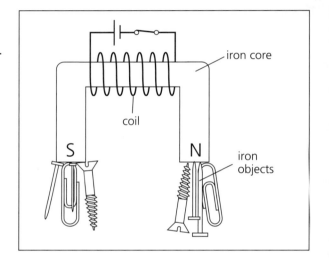

iron core

coil

iron objects

 Now do this

1 Sketch the magnetic field lines around a coil of wire which carries an electric current.

2 Name **three** things which increase the strength of an electromagnet.

A **relay** uses an electromagnet to control an electrical switch. A small current in the **coil** attracts the iron **armature**, closing the copper **contacts**. The contacts open as soon as there is no current in the coil. The current in the contacts is often large or at a dangerous voltage.

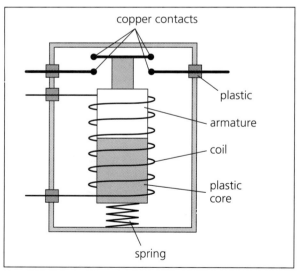

copper contacts

plastic

armature

coil

plastic core

spring

Inside a relay

 Now do this

3 Draw a labelled diagram of a relay.

4 Describe and explain how to close and open the relay contacts.

An electric **bell** uses an electromagnet.

There can only be a current in the coil if the contacts are closed. But any current in the coil will result in the armature moving towards the electromagnet, opening the contacts. So the armature moves up and down rapidly.

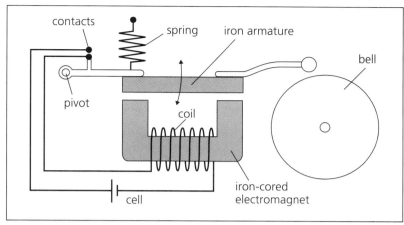

An electric bell

Now do this

5 Complete the sentences for an electric bell. Choose words from the following:

armature   open   off   close   comes on

When the contacts are closed, the electromagnet
_____ . This attracts the _____ , so
the contacts _____ . This turns the
electromagnet _____ , the armature is
pulled back by the spring and the contacts
_____ once more.

An electric motor contains a coil of copper wire inside a magnet. The coil is free to rotate on its axis. It sits in a magnetic field from a permanent magnet or an electromagnet.

Electric current in the coil interacts with the magnetic field to create a pair of forces. These act in opposite directions, forcing the coil to turn round.

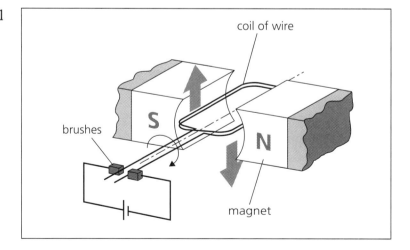

Now do this

6 Electric motors contain copper and steel. Explain what each material is used for.

7 Draw a diagram to show the forces on the coil of an electric motor.

Electricity on a large scale

Electricity is made on a large scale by boiling water to make high pressure steam. The steam passes through a turbine, making it spin round. The turbine is connected to the shaft of a generator. Coils of copper wire are attached to the shaft. The coils spin inside strong magnetic fields which generate electricity.

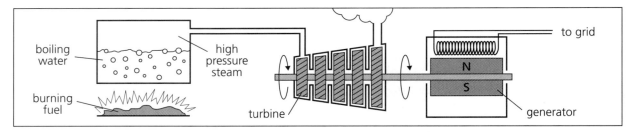

The water can be boiled by burning a fuel (such as coal, oil or gas) or by a nuclear reaction. Here is an energy flow diagram for a typical gas-fired electricity power station.

Each time the energy is transformed, some heat energy is lost. Overall, 1000 J of chemical energy in the gas becomes 400 J of electrical energy in the wires coming out of the generator. The remaining 600 J becomes heat energy at various places. The **efficiency** of the whole process can be calculated with a formula.

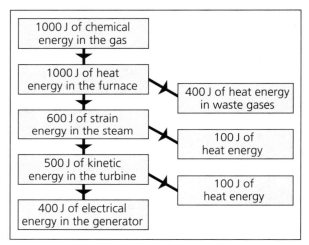

$$\text{efficiency} = \frac{\text{useful output}}{\text{input}} \times 100$$

input = 1000 J
useful output = 400 J
efficiency = ?

$$\text{efficiency} = \frac{400}{1000} \times 100 = 40\%$$

The final value for the efficiency is quoted as a percentage. This is why it is sometimes called percentage efficiency (% efficiency).

Now do this

1 Describe how electricity is generated from oil.

2 Draw an energy flow diagram for a power station.

3 Write down the formula for calculating efficiency.

4 200 J of chemical energy in coal becomes 50 J of electrical energy in a power station. Calculate the efficiency of the power station.

Transmitting electricity

Electricity is carried from power stations around the country by the National Grid, which is a network of cables. The electric current in the network generates heat energy because of the resistance of the wires to the current. This is a waste of energy and it reduces the efficiency of the network.

The efficiency is improved by keeping the current flowing through the grid at a very high voltage.

The voltage used for transmission is high so it has to be converted back into a much lower voltage for use in homes. So a **step down transformer** is used to lower the voltage of the current as it leaves the grid. **Step up transformers** are used to raise the voltage of the ac leaving the power station for the grid.

A transformer is a loop of soft iron. Alternating current (ac) in the primary coil continually changes the magnetism of the iron. This change of magnetism generates a voltage in the secondary coil. Because there are fewer loops on the secondary coil than the primary the voltage there will be lower. This process happens the other way round in a step up transformer.

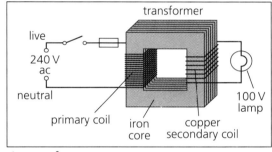

A transformer

Transformers have a very high efficiency. Very little electricity gets converted to heat energy on the way through them. They can only be used with alternating current.

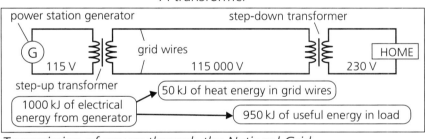

Transmission of power through the National Grid

Now do this

5 What is the National Grid? What does it do?

6 For every 1000 kJ of electricity fed into the grid, only 950 kJ can be extracted from it.
 a What happens to the missing energy?
 b Calculate the efficiency of the grid.

7 Why is the grid run at a high voltage?

8 There is always a transformer between a generator and the National Grid. What does the transformer do?

Gravity and space

Gravity

Jo drops a ball over the edge of a high cliff. **Gravity** tugs the ball downwards, towards the centre of the Earth. So the ball speeds up (accelerates).

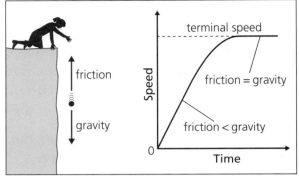

As it speeds up, friction force from the air increases until it is the same size as the gravity force. At this point the ball starts travelling at a steady speed and stays at that speed until it hits the ground. This is called the **terminal velocity** of the ball.

When the two forces have the same strength they are **balanced**. They have the same strength, but act in opposite directions.

> The acceleration of an object in free fall without friction is called *g*. It is about 10 m/s² for all objects near the Earth.

Space

The Earth we live on is one of several planets which orbit the Sun. The Sun is our nearest star and is much larger than any of the planets. Like other stars it is very hot and gives off light.

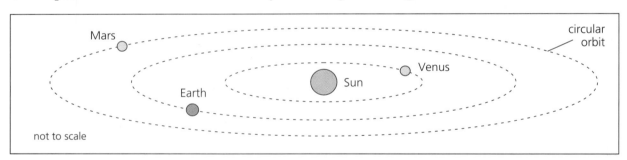

The Sun's gravity pulls on each planet and keeps it in orbit. There is no friction in space, so orbits can keep going for billions of years. The time it takes for a planet to orbit the Sun depends on how far it is from the Sun.

Now do this

1   Copy and complete these sentences. Choose from the following words:

stays the same   gravity   speed   increases   balanced   upwards   friction

When an object is released _____ acts on it, so its _____ increases. The motion through the air produces the force _____ which acts _____. The friction _____ as the speed increases. At the terminal speed, the forces are _____ and the speed _____ _____ _____.

Moons, satellites and comets

Earth has one moon. It goes round the Earth once a month and is held in orbit by Earth's gravity. A moon is a smaller lump of rock which orbits a planet. Many planets have more than one moon.

People have put satellites into orbit around Earth and these are also held in place by Earth's gravity. The orbit time of a satellite in orbit around the Earth depends on its height above the surface. The orbit time increases as the height increases.

Comets are small lumps of icy rock which have very elliptical orbits around the Sun.

The speed of comets increases as they approach the Sun, and they slow down as they move away from it.

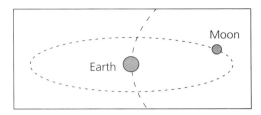

The Moon orbits the Earth which orbits the Sun

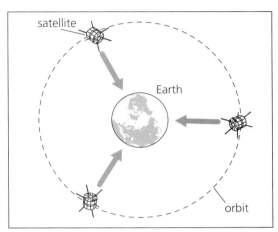

Forces on a satellite at different points in orbit around Earth.

Orbit of a comet

The universe

The Sun, its planets and their moons make up a **solar system**. There are billions of solar systems clumped together around other stars in our local galaxy, the Milky Way. The universe contains billions of different galaxies, separated by empty space.

??? Now do this

2 What is a comet?

3 Describe the path of a comet around the Sun.

4 How does the orbit time of a satellite change as its height above the Earth increases?

5 Write out the following items in order of size. Start with the smallest.

   galaxy   moon   star   solar system   universe   planet

Radioactivity

All atoms have a small nucleus made up of protons and neutrons. Electrons move around the nucleus. All the atoms in an element have the same number of protons.

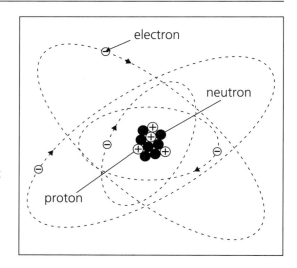

Types of radiation

Some atoms have a nucleus which is unstable. It can break up, spitting out particles which have a lot of energy. Each particle has two protons and two neutrons and is called an **alpha particle** (α). This is **alpha radiation**.

The atom left behind has lost two protons so it has become a different element.

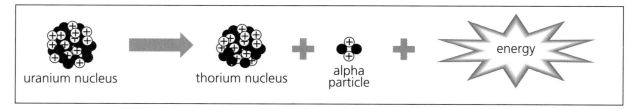

uranium nucleus → thorium nucleus + alpha particle + energy

Beta radiation is also formed from the breakdown of an unstable nucleus. This happens when one of the neutrons splits into a proton and a high energy electron. The electron whizzes out of the atom as a **beta particle**. The proton stays. As the original atom has an extra proton it turns into a new element.

Gamma radiation is not a particle at all. It is an electromagnetic wave which has no charge.

What does radiation do?

All types of radiation can pass through (**penetrate**) matter. They knock electrons out of atoms they pass through, leaving positively charged ions. This is called **ionisation**.

Ionisation is dangerous to living things. It can kill cells or change their genetic structure. Too much exposure to nuclear radiation can lead to cancer or birth defects. People who work with radiation must wear special protective clothing, use protective screens and limit the amount of time they are exposed to it.

Now do this

1 Name the radiation which:
   a has the greatest mass
   b is a wave
   c is a nucleus
   d is an electron.

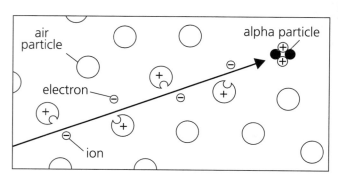

Alpha particles are the least penetrating radiation. They can be stopped by a sheet of paper. Beta particles are stopped by a few millimetres of aluminium. Gamma rays can pass through several centimetres of lead, so they are the most penetrating.

Penetration of different types of radiation

Uses of radiation

- Gamma rays are used to sterilise surgical instruments and kill cancer tumours.
- Alpha particle sources are used in smoke alarms. The alarms go off when smoke stops the flow of alpha particles inside them.
- Beta particle sources are used to measure the thickness of sheets of paper.

Background radiation

We are surrounded by **background radiation** from:
- radioactive atoms, such as uranium, in rocks
- radioactive gases, such as radon, from the soil
- fallout from nuclear bomb tests and nuclear power stations
- cosmic rays from space.

When scientists experiment with radiation they have to make allowances for background radiation in their results. It varies from place to place.

Radioactive decay

The radioactivity of a material goes down (**decays**) over time. When the last unstable nucleus has split, the material is no longer radioactive. Some materials take a very long time to decay, others are only radioactive for a short while. The age of rocks can be measured by working out how far radioactive materials in them have decayed.

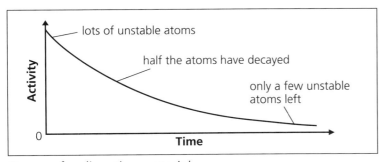

Decay of radioactive material

Now do this

2 Why would beta or gamma radiation not work in a smoke alarm?

3 Why could you not use alpha radiation to measure paper thickness?

Now do this

4 Name four sources of background radiation.

5 How does the activity of a radioactive material change with time and why?

6 State one use for
   a alpha particles
   b beta particles
   c gamma rays
   d uranium.

Gravity and weight

The force of gravity on an object is known as **weight**. It depends on both the mass of the object and the acceleration of free fall gravity. 'Free fall' means that no other force is acting on it such as an engine pushing it downwards.

weight (N) = mass (Kg) × gravity (m/s² or N/kg)

The acceleration of gravity is different on different planets. The greater the size and density of the planet, the greater its gravity. This is sometimes called its **gravitational field strength**. This means that objects with the same mass have different weights depending on where they are. On Jupiter you would weigh up to 90 times what you weigh on Earth.

The mass of an object does not depend on where it is. This is because mass is fixed by the number and type of atoms in the object.

Example

An astronaut has a weight of 800 N on Earth, where g is 10 m/s².
What is his weight on the Moon where $g = 1.6$ m/s²?

On the Earth: weight = mass × g On the Moon: weight = mass × g
            800   = mass × 10   weight = 80 × 1.6 = 128 N
            so mass = 800/10 = 80 kg

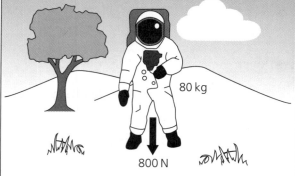
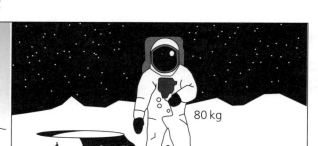

Now do this

1   Write down the formula for calculating weight from mass. What are the units of weight and mass?

2   Explain why the weight of an object depends on its location but its mass does not.

3   Telhar weighs 500 N on Earth. What are his mass and weight when he goes to Mars (where $g = 4$ m/s²)?

Moments

Sam and Jo are sitting on a plank of wood. The centre of the plank is on a pivot. Jo has a smaller weight than Sam, so she needs to sit further from the pivot to make the plank balance.

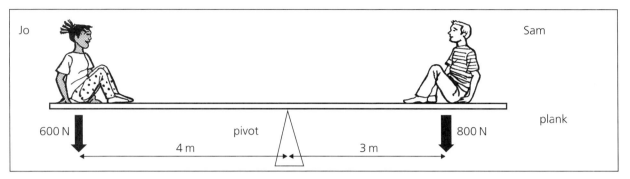

Sam provides a clockwise moment of 800 N × 3 m = 2400 Nm.

Jo must provide an anticlockwise moment of 2400 Nm for the plank to balance. Her weight is 600 N, so she must sit 4 m from the pivot (600 × 4 = 2400).

Sue pushes down on Sam's end of the plank with a force of 200 N, at a distance of 4 m from the pivot. This adds an extra clockwise moment of 200 × 4 = 800 Nm. The total clockwise moment must still be 2400 Nm for balance. So Sam has to move to 2 m from the pivot (800 N × 2 m = 1600 Nm).

Now do this

4 Calculate the values of x required for balance.

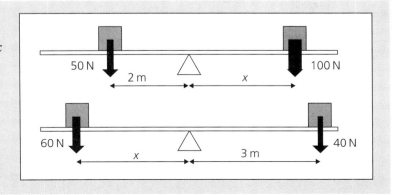

Concept map

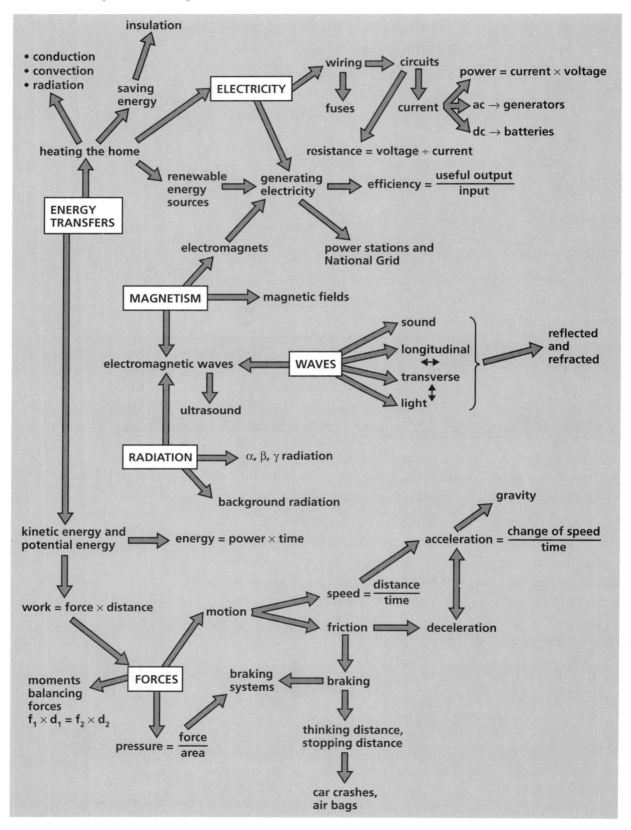

Exam questions

1 Lucy blows down a whistle.

The whistle makes a sound.

a i What makes a sound wave? [1]

ii The sound has a frequency of 2000 Hz. How many vibrations are produced in 2 s? [1]

b Here is a simple wave diagram for the sound.

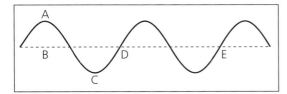

i A trough of the wave is shown by letter _____ . [1]

ii The amplitude is between letter _____ and _____ . [1]

c Rajiv blows on a different whistle. The sound has a lower frequency. What does this do to the wavelength of the sound? [1]

d Lucy is a long way from Rajiv. She sees him blow the whistle. Two seconds later, she hears the sound. Explain why. [1]

[6 marks]

2 Sanjay shines his torch on a mirror. The light reflects off the mirror. Look at the diagram.

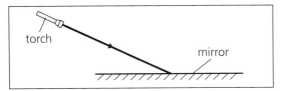

a Draw the path taken by the ray on the diagram above. [1]

b Some reflected light reaches Susan. Susan sees an image of Sanjay's torch.

Mark with an **X** on the diagram to show the position of the image. [1]

[2 marks]

3 a Here are the names of some waves.

infra-red   microwaves   radio   ultrasound   X-rays

i Which wave is longitudinal? [1]

ii Which wave has the longest wavelength? [1]

iii Which wave can cause cancer? [1]

iv Which wave can detect airplanes? [1]

v Two of the waves can be used to find broken bones. Which two? [2]

b Infra-red can pass down optical fibres. Look at the diagram.

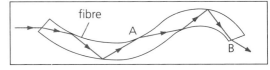

i What happens to the light at A? [1]

ii What happens to the light at B? [1]

[8 marks]

4 Tom sends a wave to Jill along a rope. Look at the diagram.

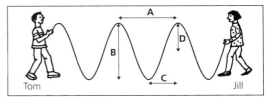

a Is the wave **longitudinal** or **transverse**? Explain how you can tell. [1]

b Which letter shows the wavelength of the wave? [1]

c Tom moves his hand up and down three times a second. State the frequency of the wave. [2]

[4 marks]

5 Freddie spends £100 a month to keep her house warm.
Look at the table.

How the heat escapes	Worth
through the windows	£10
through the floor	£15
through the roof	£25
through the walls	£35
by draughts	£15

a i Where does the least heat escape from? [1]

ii Freddie decides to save money by reducing heat lost through the roof. What is the best insulating material to put in the loft? Choose from:

**brick   wood   fibre wool
steel   tile** [1]

b Freddie draughtproofs her house. What could Freddie do to stop the draughts? [1]

c Freddie wants to save even more money on her heating bills.

Explain two ways in which she could do this. [2]

[5 marks]

6 Pete takes some ice cream out of the freezer. He puts it on the table.

a What will happen to the temperature of the ice cream? [1]

b Energy is transferred by **conduction** to the ice cream. Use the idea of particles to explain how. [3]

c Pete wraps the ice cream in shiny foil. This keeps it cold for a long time. Explain how. [2]

d Suggest what else Pete could do to keep the ice cream on the table cold for a long time. [1]

e The cooling unit of Pete's freezer is at the top. Suggest a reason why it is at the top. [1]

[8 marks]

7 Pauline is on roller blades. Look at this diagram.

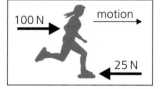

a i State what happens to Pauline's speed. [1]

ii Explain why. [1]

b Look at the diagram of three roller-bladers.

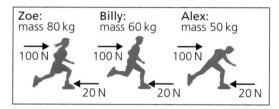

i Who will have the greatest **acceleration**? [1]

ii Explain why. [1]

[4 marks]

8 Melissa cycles from home to school. Here is the distance–time graph for her journey.

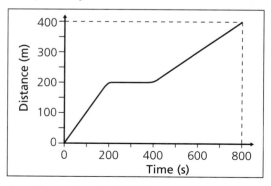

a At what time is Melissa

i not moving at all? [1]

ii moving fastest? [1]

iii accelerating? [1]

b It takes 800 s for Melissa to cycle from home to school.

  i How far does she travel in this time? [1]

  ii Calculate her average speed during the journey. [3]

c Melissa wears a cycle helmet. This will protect her if she falls off her cycle.

Complete the sentence.

Choose from: **pressure   force area   friction**

The helmet protects Melissa by spreading the _____ of a collision over a large _____ , reducing the _____ on her head to a safe value. [3]

[10 marks]

9 Here is some information from The Highway Code about stopping cars.

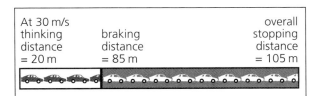

| At 30 m/s thinking distance = 20 m | braking distance = 85 m | overall stopping distance = 105 m |

a Explain what is meant by **thinking distance**. [1]

b i What happens to the thinking distance when the speed of the car is increased above 30 m/s? [1]

  ii What happens to the stopping distance if it rains? [1]

c A car at 30 m/s takes 0.7 s to travel the thinking distance and another 5.6 s to travel the braking distance.

  i How long does it take to travel the overall stopping distance? [1]

  ii Sketch a graph to show how the speed of the car changes as it stops. [3]

[7 marks]

10 Sue uses a bicycle. She pumps up the tyres.

a Here is her pump.

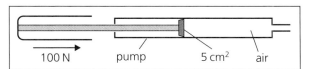

100 N   pump   5 cm²   air

The force on the piston is 100 N. The area of the piston is 5 cm². Calculate the pressure of the piston on the air. [3]

b Mike uses a pump with the same size piston.

Mike is much stronger than Sue.

Complete the sentence:

The pressure in Mike's pump is _____ because the force is _____ and the area is _____. [3]

[6 marks]

11 Look at the diagrams.

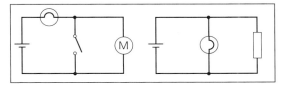

Complete the sentences.

Choose from:

become brighter   become dimmer stay the same brightness

a The switch is opened. The lamp will _____. [1]

b The resistance is increased. The lamp will _____. [1]

c Bill has one cell and two lamps. He connects them in parallel. Draw a circuit diagram to show this. [1]

d Look at the circuit diagram.

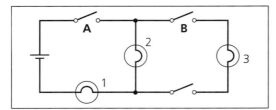

Switches A and B are pressed at the same time.
Which lamps will light? [1]
[4 marks]

12 Mel measures the power of a motor connected to a cell.

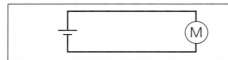

She uses a voltmeter and an ammeter.

a Draw a circuit to show this. [2]

b The voltmeter reads 1.2 V; the ammeter reads 0.6 A. Calculate
  i the power of the motor [3]
  ii the resistance of the motor. [3]
  [8 marks]

13 An LED is connected in series with a cell.

a Draw the circuit diagram. [1]

b Complete the sentences.

  Choose from: **heat light sound chemical electrical**

  _____ energy in the cell becomes _____ energy in the wires. The LED transfers _____ energy into _____ energy. [4]
  [5 marks]

14 a Jane is driving a car. She puts on the brakes.

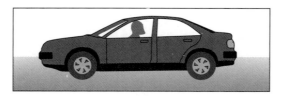

i Complete the sentence.

The brakes transfer the _____ energy of the car into _____ energy. [2]

The brakes exert a force of 500 N on the car.
It stops in a distance of 20 m.

ii Calculate the work done on the car by the brakes. [3]

b Jane pushes hard on the accelerator for 10 s.
The engine transfers 50 000 J of kinetic energy to the car.

i Calculate the power of the engine. [3]

ii 200 000 J of chemical energy was transferred into the engine during the 10 s.
Calculate the efficiency of the engine. [3]
[11 marks]

15 Look at the diagram of the electromagnet.

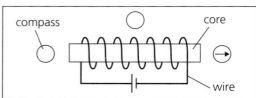

a What is the best material to use for the core? [1]

b Write down two things you could do to increase the strength of the electromagnet. [2]

c There are three compasses near the electromagnet.
The needle has been drawn for one compass.

i Draw in the other two needles. [2]

ii Write down what you could do to make the needles face in the opposite direction. [1]
[6 marks]

16 A power station burns coal to make electricity.

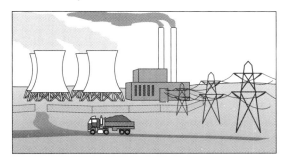

a Complete the sentences.

Choose from: **generator turbine furnace transformer boiler**

The coal is burnt in the _____.
The heat energy turns water into steam in the _____.
The steam passes through the _____ to make kinetic energy.
This is transferred to electrical energy by the _____.
The voltage of the electricity is raised by a _____. [5]

b A motor is connected to a cell.

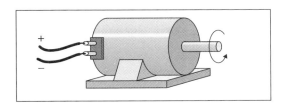

The motor shaft turns round.

i Write down what you can do to make the shaft turn the other way. [1]

ii How could you alter the circuit to make the shaft turn faster. [1]

c The motor contains some coils of wire and some magnets.

i Write down a suitable material for the wire. [1]

ii Write down a suitable material for the magnets. [1]

[9 marks]

17 Earth and Venus are planets in the Solar System.
Look at the diagram. It is not drawn to scale.
There is a star at the centre.

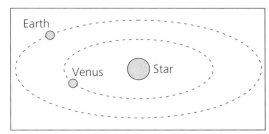

a Name the star at the centre of the Solar System. [1]

b Complete the sentences.

The Earth moves once around the star in _____.
Earth spins once on its axis in _____. [2]

c Venus is closer to the star than Earth. Compared with the Earth, what effect does this have on

i the time it takes for Venus to orbit the star [1]

ii the surface temperature of Venus. [1]

[5 marks]

18 There are satellites in orbit around the Earth.

a Name the force which keeps a satellite in orbit around the Earth. [1]

b Write down one reason why there are satellites around the Earth. [1]

[2 marks]

Page 2

2 Maggots, grass, an oak tree.

Page 3

3a chloroplasts **b** cell membrane **c** cell wall.

4 Nucleus, cytoplasm, cell membrane, mitochondria.

Page 4

1 The breakdown of large food molecules into small soluble ones.

2 Any two from: mouth, stomach, small intestine.

3 Small intestine.   4 Water.

Page 5

5 They speed up the breakdown of food.

6 Provides the right conditions for stomach enzymes to work: kills microbes in food.

7 Any two from: mouth, stomach, small intestine.

Page 7

1 Diffusion down a concentration gradient, high in the blood to low in the alveoli.

2 To be able to carry out gas exchange efficiently – transport system.

3 Rib cage lifts moving out and up; this increases the volume of the chest cavity and sucks air in.

4 The diaphragm domes upwards, the ribs are lowered therefore the volume of the chest cavity decreases; therefore air is forced out.

Page 8

1 Red blood cells.

2 To help clot the blood.

3 Capillaries, veins, arteries.

4 An artery.   5 Arteries.

Page 9

6 To pump blood around the body.

7 Right atrium, left atrium, right ventricle, left ventricle.

8 To prevent blood flowing backwards when the heart contracts.

Page 10

1 Skin – temperature and pressure; ear – sound; eye – light; nose – chemicals.

2 Iris – controls amount of light entering eye; lens; optic nerve – carries messages to brain.

Page 11

3 Stimulus (the ball), receptor (retina), sensory neurone (optic nerve), central nervous system (brain), motor neurone, effector (muscle in eye lid), response (blink).

Page 13

1 A chemical messenger.

2 Glands (endocrine glands).

3 Diabetics do not make enough insulin and insulin is needed to control blood glucose levels, therefore the insulin injections allow people with diabetes to control their glucose levels.

4a Oestrogen –
   • girls start their menstrual cycle (have periods)
   • develop breasts
   • grow pubic and underarm hair
   • grow taller.

 b Testosterone
   • boys develop longer penises
   • grow pubic, underarm and facial hair
   • develop deeper voices.

5 She maintains a high level of progesterone to keep the uterus lining in place for the baby to develop in, therefore the uterus lining cannot come away as menstruation.

6 It prevents the ovaries releasing eggs.

7 Oestrogen helps to repair and build up the lining of the uterus.

Page 14

1 Hormones have to reach their target site either by travelling in the blood or through water in plants, they then cause an effect, but this takes a lot longer than a nervous message whizzing along a nerve cell.

Page 15

2 A plant (growth) hormone.

3 Light, gravity.

4 Rooting compound; control speed of fruit ripening; selective weedkillers.

5 One which only kills certain types of plants and leaves others unharmed.

Page 16

1 Soil/compost; air.

2 Any four of the labelled organisms in the bottle garden e.g. wood louse, green fly, fern, worm, ivy.

3 All the animals would eventually die and the ecosystem would break down.

4 Any reasonable example, for example a tree, a wood, a lake, a hedge.

Page 17

5 A – pipistrelle B – buttercup
   C – tarantula D – Scot's pine E – pike.

Page 18

1 Animals – water, space, food, shelter, minerals; plants – water, space, light, minerals.

2 There is less competition for space, food, therefore the fish are not limited by their resources as much as they are in a small goldfish bowl.

3 Thick fur; thick layer of fat/blubber; large body mass.

Page 19

4 For example, tiger, stripes to break up its outline so it blends in well; sharp claws; huge teeth.

5 For example, rabbit, lives in a hole; feeds with lots of other rabbits so someone is always on guard; eyes on the side of the head to give very wide field of vision to spot predator.

6 They will decrease too because they will have nothing to eat.

7 a barn owl b more owls killed, therefore fewer field mice eaten, therefore field mice eat more of the wheat – less wheat left for farmer.

Page 20

1 a Producer – heather; primary consumer – rabbit, grouse, bees, deer; predator – fox, eagle.

  b Any two starting with heather, e.g. heather → grouse → fox.

  c Should show a normal pyramid shape.

Page 21

2 Primary consumer.

3 A food chain only shows one feeding relationship whereas a food web is more realistic and shows many more feeding relationships.

Page 22

1 Organism which breaks down waste and dead materials.

2 Fungi and bacteria.

3 They recycle nutrients which would otherwise be locked away inside dead things.

Page 23

4 Burning them releases carbon dioxide which builds up in the atmosphere upsetting the balance of the carbon cycle; they also release sulphur dioxide which gives rise to acid rain.

5 Plant material becoming fossilised over thousands of years, burning fossil fuel returning carbon dioxide to the atmosphere.

Page 25

1 It only involves one parent and therefore there is no fertilisation as gametes join.

2 A sex cell.   3 Sperm, egg.

4 The egg comes from the female and females only contain two X chromosomes, therefore they cannot put any other sex chromosome into their egg.

5 19.

Page 26

1 A change in the gene or chromosome structure.

2 Chormosomes not being copied correctly in cells; exposure to radiation; exposure to certain chemicals (mutagens).

3 Down's syndrome.

Page 27

4 a Speed. b Selective breeding – pick two speedy parents, breed them and pick the fastest foal, repeat, repeat and repeat.

Page 29

2 The remains of a dead organism which has become part of the rock.

3 Sedimentary.

4 Many years ago it had to paddle around in marshes and hide from predators, therefore it had splayed feet and was small – over millions of years the marshes dried out and the horse needed to move on hard ground, therefore it evolved a hoof and longer legs to escape its predators by running away quickly.

5 Some body parts do not fossilise; only some organisms were in the right place at the right time, some may have died and been eaten; there are still thousands which we have not yet found.

Page 30

1 They use light energy to change carbon dioxide and water into sugars (food).

2 Carbon dioxide + water $\xrightarrow[\text{and light energy}]{\text{chlorophyll}}$ glucose + oxygen

3 The atmosphere.   4 The soil.

Page 31

5 Broad; thin; lots of chlorophyll; good transport system; stomata.

6 Oxygen or water vapour or carbon dioxide – air is too vague.

7 No, because they need light to photosynthesise.

Page 32

1 Xylem – transports water and minerals; phloem – transports dissolved food (sucrose).

2 Magnesium is used to make chlorophyll which is green. Chlorophyll is also needed for photosynthesis so low chlorophyll means the plant does not make as much food and therefore does not grow so well.

3 Changed into sucrose for transport; changed into cellulose; changed into proteins; respired to release energy; changed into starch for storage.

Page 33

4 Absorb water and minerals from the soil.

5 1 Cell wall; 2 cell membrane; 3 cytoplasm; 4 vacuole 5 nucleus.

6 B.

7 Because there is a lot of water inside B and very little outside the cell, therefore water will move from a high concentration to a low concentration.

Page 35

1 a The ink travels up the xylem to the leaves with the water.

b
stained blue

2 Prevents the plant losing too much water by evaporation.

3 The evaporation of water from the leaves of a plant and its replacement by water from the xylem.

4 It provides water for photosynthesis; cools the plant down; helps to move minerals up the plant; provides support because the cells are stiff when full of water.

5 a Carbon dioxide diffuses in through open stomata.

b Oxygen diffuses out through the stomata from a high concentration to a relatively lower concentration in the atmosphere.

Page 37

1 Energy; glucose; oxygen; aerobic; anaerobic; lactic.

2 a glucose + oxygen → carbon dioxide + water + energy

b glucose → lactic acid + some energy

3 All the cells in the body.

4 Breathing rate increases; heart beat increases; aerobic respiration increases.

5 Anaerobic respiration producing ethanol and carbon dioxide.

6 glucose → ethanol + carbon dioxide + some energy

7 Breadmaking - carbon dioxide makes bread light; brewing - ethanol gives alcoholic content of beers and wines.

Page 38

1 Maintaining conditions in your body at a steady state (optimum level).

2 Pancreas and the liver.

3 Water; urea; salt.   4 Urine.

5 Lungs.

Page 39

6 Brain.

7 Sweat uses some of our body heat to evaporate it off the skin, therefore some of the body heat is used up.

8 Shivering; vasoconstriction; putting extra clothes on; plus why each one helps.

Page 41

1 Tears contain antiseptic which destroys microbes.

2 The blood blocks the hole (platelets) and white blood cells launch a counter attack.

3 A chemical produced to attack something our body recognises as foreign (antigen).

4 To reach any invading microbes so that they can launch an attack.

5 Chemicals in the smoke stop the cilia beating therefore the mucus and microbes lodges in the lungs rather than constantly being removed – here they can cause infections.

6 A drug is a substance that changes the way your body works.

7 Depressant – slows down brain activity, e.g. alcohol; stimulant – speeds up brain activity, e.g. caffeine.

Page 50

1 Particles can move through a container; particles are randomly arranged.

2 Particles are held in position and can't move closer.

Page 51

1 Hydrogen sulphide, sugar, nitric acid.

2 Salt and sand, salty water.

Page 52

1 a Evaporate.   b Filter.

c Filter, evaporate.   d Dissolve, filter, evaporate.

Page 53

2 Colourless steam.

3 Pure water.   4 In the flask.

5 Fractional distillation.

Page 54

1 a hydrogen + oxygen → hydrogen oxide
　　 reactant　　 reactant　　　　 product

　b carbon + iron oxide → carbon dioxide + iron
　　 reactant　　 reactant　　　　 product　　　 product

　c propane → hydrogen + propene
　　 reactant　　 product　　 product

2　sodium + water → sodium hydroxide + hydrogen

Page 55

3 a LHS　1 atom of Mg, 2 atoms of Cl
　　 RHS　1 atom of Mg, 2 atoms of Cl
　　 equation balances

　b LHS　1 atom of Mg, 2 atoms of O
　　 RHS　2 atoms of Mg, 2 atoms of O
　　 equation doesn't balance

　c LHS　1 atom of C, 4 atoms H *and* 4 atoms of O = 1 of C, 4 of H, 4 of O
　　 RHS　1 atom of C, 2 atoms O *and* 4 atoms H, 2 atoms O = 1 of C, 4 of H, 4 of O
　　 equation balances

Page 57

1　Increase temperature; increase concentration of acid; increase surface area by using smaller pieces of carbonate.

2　The first two.

3 a A, the slope is steepest.　　**b** C.

Page 58

1　200 °C, 100 °C, 300 °C.

2　Because it has a lower boiling point.

3　Because it has more carbon atoms.

Page 59

4　Alkanes; carbon; hydrogen; carbon dioxide; water oxidation.

5　methane + oxygen → carbon dioxide + water

Page 60

1　Fuel B.　　**2**　Exothermic.

Page 61

3　Carbon dioxide; greenhouse; ultra-violet; infra-red; sulphur dioxide.

Page 62

1　Respiration, combustion.

2　Photosynthesis.

Page 63

3　80%; 20%; 0.04%; oxygen; carbon dioxide; respiration; combustion.

Page 64

1, 2 The majority of volcanoes lie close to the edges of the plates.

3　The earthquake zones are very close.

Page 65

4 a Underneath, into the mantle.

　b The rocks melt.

5　The rocks get older.

Page 66

1　Large; igneous; metamorphic.

Page 67

2　Weathering; sedimentary; metamorphic; upthrust.

Page 68

1　zinc + copper oxide → zinc oxide + copper

2 a Copper oxide, silver oxide.

　b The metal and water will be formed.

Page 69

3　Reduction.

4　Carbon + copper oxide → carbon dioxide + copper

5 a Zinc.　　**b** Zinc is more reactive than iron.

Page 70

1　Positive.　　**2**　Negative.　　**3** Mg^{2+}.

4　The ions can't move through the solid.

5　Negative electrode (cathode).

Page 71

6 a Positive.　　**b** Negative.

7　Negative electrode (cathode).

8　Negative electrode (cathode).

Page 72

1　5.　　**2**　2.

3　Molecular structure.

4 Giant structure.

Page 73

5　3.

6 a Methane + oxygen → carbon dioxide + water

　b $CH_4 + 2O_2 → CO_2 + 2H_2O$

Page 74

1 a C_2H_6; **b** C_2H_4.

2　Styrene + styrene + styrene + styrene + styrene → poly(styrene)

Page 75

3 a Reaction goes faster.

　b Reaction stops or slows down due to enzyme damage.

4 Carbon dioxide, alcohol.

5 Winemaking, brewing.

Page 76

1 8 to 14. **2** 7. **3** 3.

4 Baking soda.

Page 77

5 Carbon dioxide. **6** Bubbles.

7 Limewater, goes cloudy.

8 Ammonium sulphate.

9 Fertilisers make microscopic plants grow which cut off the light and make everything else die.

Page 78

1 A reaction that will go in either direction.

2 Nitrogen and hydrogen.

Page 79

3 12 g, 32 g. **4** 71 g, 48 g.

5 a 17; **b** 18, **c** 40.

Page 80

1 Oxygen–18 has two more neutrons than oxygen–16.

2 26 protons; 30 neutrons.

Page 81

3 a 7 electrons **b** 2 in the first shell, 5 in the next.

4 2, 8, 1. **5** 2, 8, 8, 1.

Page 82

1 11.

2 They have two outer electrons which they lose to leave a stable shell.

3 Group 0 elements have a stable outer electron shell.

Page 83

4 sodium + water → sodium hydroxide + hydrogen

5 $2Na + 2H_2O \rightarrow 2NaOH + H_2$

Page 84

1 hydrogen + chlorine → hydrogen chloride

2 $2Na + Cl_2 \rightarrow 2NaCl$

Page 85

1 They all have a stable outer shell.

2 Krypton is denser. **3** In lights.

Page 86

1 a B and D. **b** A and C.

Page 94

1 25 cm. **2** 3. **3** 4 m.

Page 95

4 Vibrations; frequency; hertz or Hz; longitudinal; energy flow.

Page 97

1 60°, 30°.

2 Angle of incidence is the same as the angle of reflection.

3 When their speed changes.

Page 98

1 47 Hz, 900 Hz, 12 000 Hz, 24 kHz, 50 000 Hz. The last two.

2 Looking inside people, breaking kidney stones.

Page 99

3 a Radio, microwaves, infra-red, visible light.

  b Ultra-violet, X-rays, gamma-rays.

  c Microwaves, infra-red.

  d Microwaves, radio.

Page 100

1 a –20°C **b** Conduction, convection and radiation.

2 Kinetic; vibrate; energy; conduction.

Page 101

3 a Lose energy. **b** Air at the top cools, shrinks and falls. It is replaced by a flow of hot air from the base of the fridge.

4 The currents carry hot water upwards through the cold water, mixing it up thoroughly.

5 Bad; bad; good; good.

6 Temperature goes down.

7 Particles with the most energy leave, so those left have less energy.

Page 102

1 Cheap to install, no waste gases.

2 Fuel is cheap, more efficient use of natural resources.

3 Wood (from plants).

4 Solar, wind, biomass, tidal, hydroelectric.

Page 103

5 5 years.

6 Insulator; air; conductor; metal.

Page 104

1 60 p. **2** 37.5 p.

Page 105

3 Live (brown), neutral (blue), earth (green and yellow).

4 Cuts off the current if it gets large enough to heat up the wires.

5 To the metal outside. It stops the outside becoming live and killing someone.

6 Double insulated appliances.

Page 106

1 20 m/s. 2 300 m/s.

3 1.67 m/s. 4 30.6 m/s.

Page 107

5

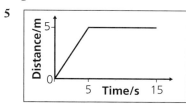

6 a = 2, **b** = 3, **c** = 1

7 a

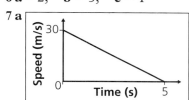

b 75 m.

Page 108

1 acceleration = change of speed/time taken

2 m/s^2 3 10 m/s^2.

4 Air resistance, contact between tyres and road, moving parts in the wheels.

5 Steady speed, getting faster, slowing down.

Page 109

6 The empty van has a smaller mass than a full one.

7 Distance moved before the brakes start to slow the car down. Lack of concentration, tiredness, intoxication.

8 Distance moved while the brakes are on. Incorrect adjustment, rain, bald tyres, badly inflated tyres.

Page 110

1 Force; length; longer; elastic; inelastic; force.

Page 111

2 Crumple zones absorb kinetic energy. Seat belts slow people down securely. Air bags provide a soft cushion.

Page 112

1 pressure = force/area 2 N, m^2, Pa.

3 $P = F/A$, P is pressure, F is force and A is area.

4 50 000 Pa. 5 16 000 Pa.

Page 113

6 Force; area; pressure; pressure.

7 2500 N.

Page 114

1 Insulator, electrons, comb, charged.

2 Becomes negative.

Page 115

3 Attract, attract, repel.

4 Photocopiers, paint sprayers.

5 The car discharges itself through you.

Page 116

1 Parallel; 6; series; battery.

Page 117

2 They both read 2 A. 3 2 A.

4 60 W.

5

─┤├─ cell	─(A)─ ammeter
─°9 v°─ power supply	─(V)─ voltmeter
	─(M)─ motor
─(⊗)─ lamp	─⊏⊞⊐─ heater

Page 118

1 B 2 resistance = voltage/current.

3 R (Ω), V (V), I (A) 4 $R = V/I$

Page 119

5 48 Ω

6 Look at the graphs on this page.

7 Look at the figure above.

8 Thermistor. 9 LDR.

Page 120

1 work = force × distance

2 W (J), F (N), s (m) 3 $W = Fs$

4 75 J, 75 J. 5 500 J

Page 121

6 Chemical; potential; potential; kinetic; heat.

7 power = work/time

8 P (W), W (J), t (S) 9 $P = W/t$ 10 200 W.

Page 122

1 Attract, attract, repel, ignore.

2 Iron, steel, cobalt, nickel.

3 North. 4 Left.

Page 123

5 a −0.1 V b 0V

6 Move the wire faster, use stronger magnets.

7 Steel for the magnets, copper for the coils which spin inside the magnets.

Page 124

1 Look at the first figure on page 124.

2 More coils, an iron core, more current.

3 Look at the figure above this question.

4 The contacts only close when you put a current in the coil.

Page 125

5 Comes on; armature; open; off; close.

6 Steel for the magnets, copper for the coils of wire.

7 Look at the figure above the question.

Page 126

1 Oil is burnt to make steam from water. The steam rotates the turbine. The turbine rotates the generator to make electricity.

2 Chemical energy in the fuel → heat energy in the steam → kinetic energy in the turbine → electrical energy in the generator.

3 efficiency = (useful output/input) × 100

4 25%.

Page 127

5 Wires which carry electricity away from power stations.

6 Heat energy, 95%.   7 To increase efficiency.

8 Increases the voltage.

Page 128

1 Gravity; speed; friction; upwards; increases; balanced; stays the same.

Page 129

2 A lump of icy rock in orbit around the Sun.

3 Elliptical.   4 Increases.

5 Moon, planet, star, solar system, galaxy, universe.

Page 130

1 a Alpha.   b Gamma.   c Alpha.   d Beta.

Page 131

2 Both penetrate the smoke too easily.

3 They won't go through the paper.

4 Uranium in rocks, radon in the air, nuclear fallout from bomb tests, cosmic rays from space.

5 Goes down, as the number of unstable atoms decreases.

6 a smoke alarms   b thickness measurement
  c sterilising instruments, killing cancers
  d generating electricity.

Page 132

1 Weight (N) = mass (kg) × gravity (m/s^2)

2 The value of gravity depends on which planet you are on. Mass only depends on the amount and type of atoms.

3 Mass = 50 kg, weight = 200 N.

Page 133

4 1 m, 2 m.

AT2

Question			Answer	Marks	Total
1	a		Nucleus.	1	
	b		To control the activities of the cell/contain the hereditary information of the cell.	1	
	c		B. It has a cell wall/it has a vacuole/it has chloroplasts.	2	**4 marks**
2	a		Diaphragm – flattens to increase the volume of the chest cavity when breathing in.	1	
			Intercostal muscles – contract to raise the ribs when breathing in.	1	
			Trachea – carries air into and out of the lungs.	1	
	b	i	Diffusion.	1	
		ii	Thin walls; moist; large surface area; good blood supply.	3	**7 marks**
3	a		Breakdown of large food molecules; into smaller, soluble ones; which can be absorbed.	2	
	b		Amino acids; maltose/sugars; fatty acids and glycerol.	4	
	c		Large surface area; thin walls; good blood supply.	2	**8 marks**
4	a		Use a water bath.	1	
	b		Respiration.	1	
	c		In **A** the coloured water will move towards the flask; as the carbon dioxide produced by the respiring maggots is absorbed by the soda lime; in **B** the coloured water will not move.	3	**5 marks**
5	a		**A** is used for sexual reproduction.	1	
			B is used to support the plant.	1	
			C is used to anchor the plant in the soil/to absorb water/minerals into the plant.	1	
	b	i	Water; oxygen.	2	
		ii	By diffusion; through the stomata.	2	
		iii	Converted into protein; converted into cellulose; converted into starch for storage; converted into sucrose for transport; used to release energy to keep the plant alive.	3	
		iv	Photosynthesis uses sunlight as the energy to produce glucose therefore there will be more of it on a sunny day, so more photosynthesis will occur; reactions are speeded up by warmer temperatures and therefore the photosynthesis reaction will occur more rapidly on a hot day, due to the higher temperature.	2	**12 marks**
6	a		lost 1.8 lost 0.3 lost 0.0	1/1/1	
	b		Water.	1	
	c		Water is lost from the stomata; Vaseline blocks the stomata and stops water loss; there is no water loss in the leaf with all the stomata blocked by Vaseline; the greatest loss is from the leaf with all its stomata free; the underside has more stomata so the leaf with a Vaseline covered bottom loses less water than the leaf with a Vaseline covered top only.	2	**6 marks**

Question	Answer	Marks	Total
7 a	Epidermis – protects the stem and reduces water loss.	1	
	Phloem – transports the products of photosynthesis/sucrose/glucose around the plant.	1	
	Xylem – transports water/dissolved minerals throughout the plant.	1	
b	Transpiration.	1	
c	Used for photosynthesis; to transport dissolved materials; to keep the plant stiff (turgid); to keep the plant cool.	2	**6 marks**
8	Iris – controls the amount of light entering the eye.	1	
	Lens – bends the light so it can be focused.	1	
	Optic nerve – carries messages to the brain.	1	
	Retina – contains light sensitive cells which respond to the incoming light.	1	**4 marks**
9 a	Right ventricle. **b** A	1 1	
c	E – towards the heart. F – away from the heart	1 1	
d	Prevents blood flowing backwards from the left ventricle to the left atrium when the ventricle contracts.	2	
e	Muscle.	1	**7 marks**
10 a	All the arrow heads point towards the right hand side of the page.	2	
b	Brain (hypothalamus),	1	
c	Sweating; sweat uses heat from the body to evaporate.	2	
	Vasodilation/opening up of the blood vessels near the surface of the skin; heat is lost by radiation to the air outside.	2	**7 marks**
11 a i	Dandelion → caterpillar → blue tit → sparrow hawk.	1	
	Dandelion → caterpillar → robin → sparrow hawk.	1	
	(All **four** organisms must be in the right order and the arrows must point in the right direction.)		
	ii Hedgehog/fox/blue tit/robin/sparrow hawk.	1	
	iii Grass/wheat/dandelion.	1	
	iv Hedgehog/fox/blue tit/robin/sparrow hawk.	2	
b	The sparrow hawks will decrease in number; they starve; there are fewer robins and blue tits for them to eat; fewer caterpillars therefore fewer robins and blue tits.	2	**8 marks**
12 a	A **c** □ blue tit / caterpillars / cabbage	1 2	
b	C	1	**4 marks**
13 a i	Chemicals which kill weeds.	1	
ii	Chemicals which kill pest animals.	1	
iii	They contain nitrates; which enable plants to make the proteins needed to grow.	2	
b i	(Graph)	3	
ii	2.5 kg per m²; adding more will cost more for the extra fertiliser, but will not cause the yield to increase any more.	2	
iii	They may remain on the foods and then get into the food chain; they may leach into the waterways; where they can cause eutrophication/death of the waterways.	2	**11 marks**

Question			Answer			Marks	Total
14			Sperm duct – carries sperm from the testes to the urethra.			2	
			Testis – where the sperm are made.			2	
			Scrotum – sac which holds the testes; keeps them at the correct temperature for healthy sperm production.			2	
			Urethra – carries urine and semen out of the body.			2	
			Penis – enables semen to be deposited inside the female.			2	**10 marks**
15	a		Nucleus.　　**b**　　To carry the genes/genetic information.			1 1	
	c		23　　**d**　　They have an extra chromosome.			1 1	
	e		**XY**			1	**5 marks**
16	a		Good mother/large litter size/good milk yield/good quality meat/good fleece.			2	
	b		Good yield/disease resistance/early cropping/able to withstand low temperature/lack of water or some other environmental condition.			2	**4 marks**
17	a		Fertilisation.　　**b**　Zygote.　　**c**　In the oviducts.			1 1 1	
	d		It divides repeatedly/it moves down into the uterus/it embeds in the uterine wall/it develops into the foetus.			1	**4 marks**
18	a		It has claws; it has legs; it does not have a backbone.　　**b**　Prawn.			3 1	**4 marks**
19	a		Large claws to grab the prey with; large beak to tear prey apart; good eyesight to locate prey; powerful wings to chase prey.			3	
	b		Live underground out of sight; feed at dusk; feed in groups so there are always lookouts; large ears to hear danger; large eyes on the side of the head to give a wide range of vision whilst feeding.			2	**5 marks**
20	a		(Graph)			2	
	b		We are becoming aware of the problem of pollution and are using less sulphur dioxide producing substances, e.g. burning less solid fuel; industry is cleaning up its act.			1	
	c		Acid rain kills germinating seeds; it destroys living trees; it attacks certain building materials; it can irritate asthma or other bronchial conditions if inhaled; it removes minerals from the soil by dissolving them out.			2	**5 marks**
21	a		(Graph)			3	
	b		Alcohol affects the brain and therefore reduces concentration/co-ordination/ability to judge distances.			1	
	c		It can cause liver damage due to constantly using the liver to break down the alcohol; the liver is vital to life therefore if the damage is too severe it results in death; or it can cause heart problems due to the conversion of alcohol into fats; this may lead to heart failure.			2	
	d	i	A substance which alters the way the body works.			1	
		ii	Any sensible suggestion, e.g. nicotine, aspirin, paracetamol, caffeine, heroin.			2	**9 marks**
22	a		Pasta; sausages.			2	
	b		$2 \times 1200 = 2400$ 　　 940 $270 + 135 = 405$ 　　 3745 kJ			2	**4 marks**

AT3

Question			Answer	Marks	Total
1	a		H_2; CH_4; S_8; H_2O **b** He; H_2; S_8 **c** CH_4; H_2O.	1 1 1	**3 marks**
2	a		B	1	
	b	i	It will go in.	1	
		ii	Particles are far apart, so can be pushed closer together.	1 1	
	c	i	Plunger will not go in.	1	
		ii	Particles close together so cannot be pushed any closer.	1 1	**7 marks**
3	a		It gives out light.	1	
	b		calcium + oxygen → calcium oxide (*one mark for the reactants, one mark for the product*)	2	
	c		$2Ca + O_2 → 2CaO$ (*one mark for the reactants, one mark for the product*)	2	**5 marks**
4	a		Rose up the filter paper. **b** No, the spots are different.	1 1	
	c	i	2 **ii** 3	1 1	**4 marks**
5	a		They have different boiling points.	1	
	b	i	Oxidation. **ii** Carbon dioxide and water.	1 2	
		iii	Carbon monoxide and water.	2	
	c		Cracking. **d** C	1 1	
	e		E-E-E-E-E-E-E-E-E-E-E-E-E-E-E-E-E-E	1	**9 marks**
6	a		26 °C **b** 38 °C	1 1	
	c		Exothermic. **d** joules or kilojoules. **e** Rise in temperature.	1 1 1	**5 marks**
7	a		Collisions	1	
			greater surface area/more places for collision	1	
	b		Collisions	1	
			particles move faster/have more energy/collide more often	1	
	c		Increase the concentration; use a catalyst.	2	**6 marks**
8	a		Igneous. **b** Rock A, it has small crystals.	1 1	
	c		Plate split, and the two halves moved apart.	2	**4 marks**
9	a		Iron, copper, silver, gold. **b** Oxygen.	2 1	**3 marks**
10	a	i	Crude oil.	1	
		ii	To make nitric acid *or* fertiliser *or* explosives.	2	
		iii	Wages, raw materials, energy, building the factory, etc.	3	
	b	i	A substance which speeds up a reaction and can be recovered.	2	
		ii	Iron.	1	
	c		The reaction will go in either (and both) direction.	1	
	d	i	About 40%.	1	
		ii	Cost of compressors or need for thicker walled reaction vessel.	1	**12 marks**
11	a	i	38 **ii** Two neutrons.	1 2	
	b		Strontium and calcium are in the same group	1	
			so will have very similar properties.	1	**5 marks**

Question			Answer	Marks	Total
12	a	i	Between 9 and 14 ii 7 iii Between 6 and 4.	1 1 1	
	b		Salt.	1	
	c	i	3 ii 3 iii 98	1 1 1	
	d		Gets into rivers and lakes. Causes eutrophication.	1 1	**9 marks**
13	a	i	Bottom of group 1. ii Top of group 7.	2 2	
	b		They have a stable outer shell or they have eight electrons in the outer shell.	1	
	c	i	2 ii 6	1 1	
	d		Double; positive.	2	**9 marks**
14	a		Ions. b To dissolve the aluminium oxide.	1 1	
	c		Ions can travel through the liquid but not the solid.	1	
	d	i	Anode. ii Cathode.	1 1	
		iii	They go to the cathode and turn into atoms (they are neutralised).	1 1	**7 marks**
15	a	i	Sugar, moisture, warmth. ii Alcohol (ethanol).	3 1	
	b	i	Speeds up the reaction. ii It can be recovered.	1 1	
	c		Carbon dioxide gas.	1	
	d		Speeds up; maximum rate at 37 °C, then slows down and stops as the yeast is killed.	4	**11 marks**
16	a	i	Sulphur dioxide. ii Sulphur + oxygen → sulphur dioxide	1 2	
		iii	Attacks stonework on buildings. Harms forests (affects the ions in the soil and streams).	2	
	b	i	Oxidation. ii Greenhouse effect.	1 1	
		iii	Raises temperatures. iv Sugars (then starch) *or* carbohydrate.	1 1	
		v	Coal. vi 0.04 %	1 1	**11 marks**

AT4

Question			Answer	Marks	Total
1	a	i	Vibration. ii 4000	1 1	
	b	i	C ii A and B	1 1	
	c		Makes it larger.	1	
	d		Light waves move much faster than sound waves.	1	**6 marks**
2	a			1	
	b			1	**2 marks**
3	a	i	Ultrasound. ii Radio. iii X-rays. iv Microwaves.	1 1 1 1	
		v	Ultrasound, X-rays.	2	
	b	i	Total internal reflection. ii Refraction.	1 1	**8 marks**
4	a		Transverse because movement of rope is at right angles to energy flow of wave.	1	
	b		A c 3 Hz	1 2	**4 marks**

Question			Answer	Marks	Total
5	a	i	Through the windows. **ii** Fibre wool.	1 1	
	b		Fill gaps around doors and windows.	1	
	c		Lower the temperature of her house.	1	
			Fill the wall cavity with insulation.	1	**5 marks**
6	a		Rise to room temperature.	1	
	b		Particles in the table are vibrating rapidly. They pass this vibration to particles they touch until all the particles are vibrating rapidly.	3	
	c		Silver foil is a poor absorber of heat radiation so it takes longer for enough energy to be absorbed to warm the ice cream.	2	
	d		Wrap it in some fluffy insulating material.	1	
	e		Cold air sinks, so all the items in the freezer are cooled.	1	**8 marks**
7	a	i	Increases. **ii** Because more force in direction of motion.	1 1	
	b	i	Alex. **ii** Because she has the smallest mass.	1 1	**4 marks**
8	a	i	Between 200 s and 400 s. **ii** Up to 200 s. **iii** At 400 s.	1 1 1	
	b	i	400 m **ii** Speed = distance/time, 0.5 m/s.	1 3	
	c		Force, area, pressure.	3	**10 marks**
9	a		The distance moved between deciding to brake and the car starting to slow down.	1	
	b	i	It increases. **ii** It increases.	1 1	
	c	i	6.3 s **ii**	1 3	**7 marks**
10	a		pressure = force/area, 20 N/cm^2 **b** Greater, greater, the same.	3 3	**6 marks**
11	a		Become dimmer. **b** Become dimmer.	1 1	
	c		**d** 1, 2.	1 1	**4 marks**
12	a			2	
	b	ii	power = voltage × current, 0.72 W	3	
		iii	resistance = voltage/current, 2 Ω	3	**8 marks**
13	a		**b** chemical, electrical, electrical, light.	1 4	**5 marks**
14	a	i	Kinetic, heat. **ii** work = force × distance, 10 000 J	2 3	
	b	i	power = energy/time, 5 000 W	3	
		ii	efficiency = (work out/work in) × 100, 25%	3	**11 marks**

Question			Answer	Marks	Total
15	a		Iron.	1	
	b		Increase the current, wrap more coils of wire.	2	
	c	i		2	
		ii	Reverse the current in the wire.	1	6 marks
16	a		Furnace, boiler, turbine, generator, transformer.	5	
	b	i	Swap over the cell connections.	1	
		ii	Put more cells in series.	1	
	c	i	Copper.	1	
		ii	Steel.	1	9 marks
17	a		Sun.	1	
	b		A year, a day.	2	
	c	i	Less time than Earth.	1	
		ii	Warmer than Earth.	1	5 marks
18	a		Gravity.	1	
	b		Communications.	1	2 marks

Index